THE YOUNG OXFORD LIBRARY OF SCIENCE

Land, Sea and Air

Margaret Carruthers

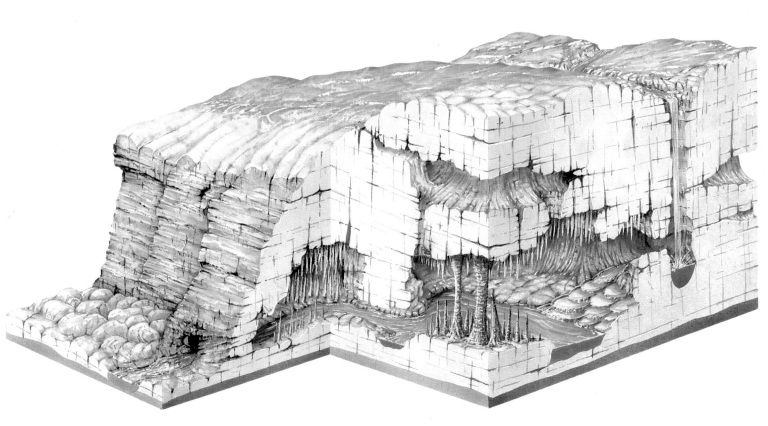

OXFORD
UNIVERSITY PRESS

OXFORD
UNIVERSITY PRESS

Great Clarendon Street, Oxford OX2 6DP

Oxford University Press is a department of the University of Oxford.
It furthers the University's objective of excellence in research, scholarship,
and education by publishing worldwide in

Oxford New York

Auckland Bangkok Buenos Aires Cape Town Chennai
Dar es Salaam Delhi Hong Kong Istanbul Karachi
Kolkata Kuala Lumpur Madrid Melbourne Mexico City Mumbai
Nairobi São Paulo Shanghai Singapore Taipei Tokyo Toronto

with an associated company in Berlin

Oxford is a registered trade mark of Oxford University Press
in the UK and in certain other countries

British Library Cataloguing in Publication Data available

Hardback ISBN 0-19-910944-3
Paperback ISBN 0-19-910945-1

1 3 5 7 9 10 8 6 4 2

Designed and typeset by Full Steam Ahead
Printed in Malaysia.

CONTENTS

THE BLUE PLANET

Four and a half billion years ago our Solar System was just a cloud of dust and gas floating among the stars. Then the cloud began to collapse, and the dust and gas spiralled inward. Most of it fell into the centre and became a star called the Sun. But some of the dust particles that were spinning around the Sun began to stick to each other, and formed large chunks of rock. These chunks joined together and grew until they became rocky planets. One of these planets was the Earth.

The Earth is the third planet from the Sun. It is the only planet in our Solar System with oceans, and it is these that make the Earth look blue from space. The Earth is the only planet where water can be found as a liquid, a solid and a gas. So the Earth has ice caps and glaciers, and water vapour in the air, as well as oceans, lakes and rivers. And, as far as we know, the Earth is the only planet with living things on it.

The changing Earth

The Earth's surface is changing all the time. Water breaks rocks and moves them from place to place. The continents slowly come together and rip apart. And living things change the Earth's surface.

   Everything we see on Earth today is the result of billions of years of changes by heat, water, air, gravity and life. The Earth was very different when it was young. When the Earth first formed it was so hot that the

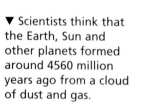

key words
- atmosphere
- crust
- mantle
- outer and inner core

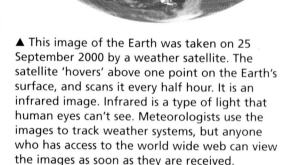

▲ This image of the Earth was taken on 25 September 2000 by a weather satellite. The satellite 'hovers' above one point on the Earth's surface, and scans it every half hour. It is an infrared image. Infrared is a type of light that human eyes can't see. Meteorologists use the images to track weather systems, but anyone who has access to the world wide web can view the images as soon as they are received.

surface was an ocean of liquid rock. Light parts floated to the surface where they cooled and hardened into the crust. The heavier parts sank to the centre and formed the Earth's core. The mantle formed in between the light crust and the dense core.

   Because the Earth was so hot there were many more volcanoes. Gases erupted from the volcanoes and formed the Earth's atmosphere. One of the gases was water vapour, which rained out to the form the oceans.

▼ Scientists think that the Earth, Sun and other planets formed around 4560 million years ago from a cloud of dust and gas.

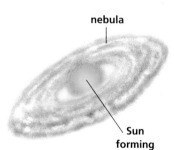

1. The Solar System began as a rotating cloud of gas and dust (a nebula).

nebula

Sun forming

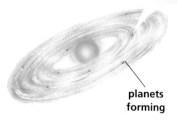

2. Most of the gas and dust formed the Sun. Around the Sun the planets formed, one of which was Earth.

planets forming

3. At first, **the Earth was so hot** that its surface was almost all molten.

Earth

4. Over time, **the Earth cooled.** A crust of hard rock formed, and water vapour condensed from the air to form oceans.

Exploring the Earth's insides

It is impossible to drill all the way through the Earth and actually see what's inside, so we have to explore it in other ways. When rocks on the Earth's surface erode (wear away), other rocks from deep in the crust are exposed on the surface, and we can study them. Volcanoes sometimes bring up rocks from even deeper down. Geologists can also find out about the inner layers of the Earth by studying earthquakes and meteorites.

If you were actually able to travel through the Earth, you would notice that the deeper you go, the hotter the rocks get. At the centre of the Earth the temperature is probably about 4500°C. You would also notice that the rocks become denser as you go down. They are made of heavier elements and they are being squashed tightly by the weight of all the rocks above.

▲ This is what Earth would look like without oceans hiding the seafloor. As on the land, there are high mountain ranges, deep valleys, and flat plains on the ocean floor.

INSIDE THE EARTH

The Earth isn't the same all the way through. It is made of five different layers – the atmosphere, crust, mantle, outer core, and inner core.

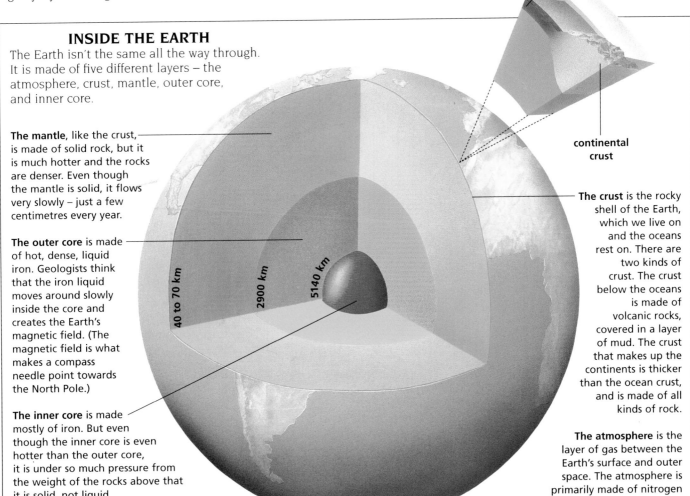

The mantle, like the crust, is made of solid rock, but it is much hotter and the rocks are denser. Even though the mantle is solid, it flows very slowly – just a few centimetres every year.

The outer core is made of hot, dense, liquid iron. Geologists think that the iron liquid moves around slowly inside the core and creates the Earth's magnetic field. (The magnetic field is what makes a compass needle point towards the North Pole.)

The inner core is made mostly of iron. But even though the inner core is even hotter than the outer core, it is under so much pressure from the weight of the rocks above that it is solid, not liquid.

ocean crust

atmosphere

continental crust

The crust is the rocky shell of the Earth, which we live on and the oceans rest on. There are two kinds of crust. The crust below the oceans is made of volcanic rocks, covered in a layer of mud. The crust that makes up the continents is thicker than the ocean crust, and is made of all kinds of rock.

The atmosphere is the layer of gas between the Earth's surface and outer space. The atmosphere is primarily made of nitrogen and oxygen.

40 to 70 km

2900 km

5140 km

PORTRAITS OF THE EARTH

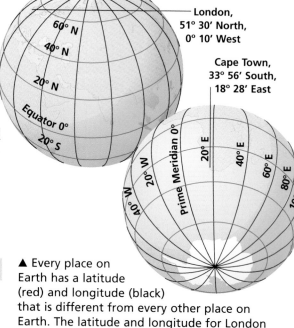

▲ Every place on Earth has a latitude (red) and longitude (black) that is different from every other place on Earth. The latitude and longitude for London and Cape Town are shown in degrees (°) and minutes ('). (There are 60 minutes in a degree.)

When most people think of maps, they think of the road maps they use to find their way around, or political maps that show where countries, cities and towns are in the world. You can actually make a map of just about anything, from the galaxies in the Universe to the ant hills in your back garden.

A map is a drawing or an image of a place that highlights specific information about the area.

There are many different kinds of map. Physical relief maps show the shape of the land, by marking land at different elevations (heights) above sea level. The map of South Africa on the opposite page is of this type. Geological maps (such as the one below) show what rocks are on the Earth's surface or just beneath the soil. Climate maps show how climates vary from one part of the world to another.

key words

- elevation
- latitude and longitude
- meridian
- parallel
- physical relief map
- political map
- projection

Latitude and longitude

To make it easier to describe where things are on the Earth, people have divided the surface into a grid. Longitude lines, also known as meridians, run from the North Pole to the South Pole. Latitude lines, also called parallels, are like rings around the Earth that run parallel to the Equator.

Latitude and longitude are measured in *degrees* rather than kilometres or miles. Latitude is measured in degrees north or south of the equator. Longitude is measured in degrees east or west of the Prime Meridian. The Prime Meridian is the line of longitude that runs through Greenwich, England.

Maps for all occasions

It would be confusing (and impossible) to put every bit of information about a place on one map, so we have hundreds of kinds of maps.

People use maps for many things. For example, hikers use topographic maps to plan their routes. Mining companies use geological maps to decide where to explore for important minerals. Meteorologists make weather maps every three hours in order to track storms and other weather systems.

◀ This is a geological map of England, Wales and part of Scotland. Geologists use such maps to work out the geological history of a particular place, to plan building projects, and to find important natural resources such as coal.

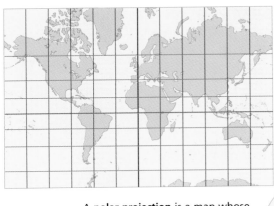

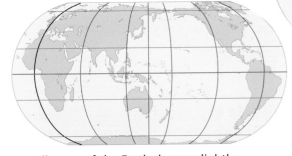

▲ All maps of the Earth show a slightly distorted view. The problem is that the Earth is a sphere, but maps are flat. People have developed different kinds of maps for different uses. Each is accurate in some ways and distorted in other ways.

A **polar projection** is a map whose centre is at the North or the South pole. The shapes of things are right, but things at the edge of the map look bigger than they really are.

Mercator projections are useful for navigating because the directions are not distorted. But things at the north and south edges look much bigger than they really are.

In an **Eckert projection**, the scale of the areas is the same everywhere on the map. However, both the shapes and directions are distorted.

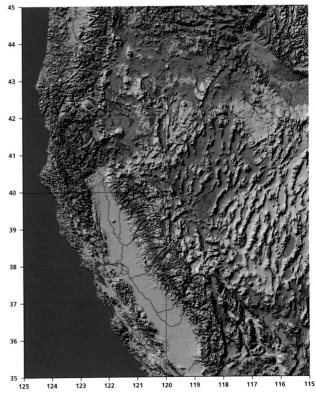

▲ This Digital Elevation Model (DEM) shows part of the western USA: the long, flat, green strip is the Central Valley of California. Such images are made using computer programs that put together millions of elevation (height) measurements taken from aircraft, satellites and surveyors on the ground. Each colour represents a different elevation.

READING MAPS

The map on the right is a topographical (physical relief) map of South Africa. To read this map, you need to know which direction is which, how big an area is shown, and what the symbols mean.

As on most maps, north is towards the top, with west to the left, east to the right and south towards you. Sometimes there is an arrow pointing north to remind you.

To show how big an area is shown, there is a scale bar. This shows that every centimetre on the map represents 16 million centimetres (160 kilometres) on the ground.

The different elevations (heights) above sea level are shown in different colours on the map. The key (or legend) tells you what the different colours mean. It also shows what the symbols used on the map mean.

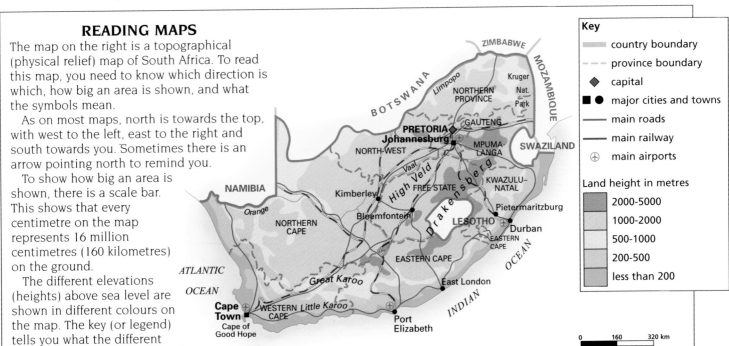

Key
- country boundary
- province boundary
- ◆ capital
- ■ ● major cities and towns
- main roads
- main railway
- ✈ main airports

Land height in metres
- 2000-5000
- 1000-2000
- 500-1000
- 200-500
- less than 200

THE SCIENCE OF THE EARTH

To a geologist, a piece of sandstone is not just a rock. It is part of an ancient beach or desert. Its sand particles were once part of a mountain. The sandstone could be used to build a house or it may hold oil that could be used for energy. It might contain the bones of an extinct animal, or imprints of an ancient plant that could tell us about the Earth's history.

Geology is the study of the Earth – what it is made of, how it formed, how it has changed, and how it is changing today.

Detective work

Geologists use many tools to understand the Earth, but the most important tools are their powers of observation and reasoning. They watch rivers flow, carefully observe rock formations, and analyse minerals under a microscope. After gathering all the evidence, they form theories about how the Earth formed and how it changes over time.

When geologists see limestone full of fossils, they know that the ground they are standing on must have once been a shallow, tropical sea. Limestone forms today in shallow tropical seas, so it must have formed there in the past. Geologists work out how rocks formed millions of years ago by watching them form today.

▶ This geologist is measuring the temperature of a recent lava flow from a volcano.

key words
- geology

Different kinds of geologist

Geologists study different parts of the Earth for many different reasons. Some study volcanoes so that they can predict eruptions. Some search for deposits of important minerals like copper and gold. There are geologists who help engineers by making sure the rocks are stable enough to build on, and others who look for water underground. Many geologists study rocks just because they are interested in how the Earth formed.

▼ James Hutton (1726–1797) inspecting the rocks near his home in Edinburgh, Scotland. Hutton is called the 'father of modern geology'. In his time most people concluded from the Bible that the Earth was only 6000 years old. By watching the forces that destroyed old rocks and created new ones, Hutton reasoned that the Earth must be millions of years old.

THE BUILDING BLOCKS OF ROCKS

Deep underground, hot, liquid rock is turning solid. As it cools, atoms of silicon and oxygen are attaching to each other, creating quartz. At the surface a salty lake is drying up and tiny cubes of salt are forming from the sodium and chlorine in the water.

Quartz and salt are both minerals. Minerals are the building blocks of rocks. Every mineral has a specific chemical make-up. For example, every crystal of quartz contains two atoms of oxygen for every atom of silicon. Every molecule of salt is made of one sodium atom and one chlorine atom. Rocks such as granite, however, are not minerals. There is no single recipe for granite.

⬤ **key words**

- crystal
- element
- mineral
- rock

diamond

◀ ▲ Different minerals can grow from the same elements depending on where they form. Near the Earth's surface, carbon atoms make soft, black, sooty-looking graphite. But 100 km deep in the Earth's mantle where the pressures are high, the same carbon atoms form hard, clear diamonds.

Crystals of all shapes and sizes

Every mineral has a crystalline structure. This means that all of the atoms and molecules in the mineral are arranged in a particular three-dimensional pattern. Some minerals, such as quartz, form large crystals that we can see. In other minerals the crystals are too small to see with the naked eye.

Identifying minerals

Geologists can identify most minerals by properties such as colour, shape, hardness, density and the way they break. Gold is easy to tell from fool's gold (the mineral pyrite) because it is much denser and softer. Salt breaks into cubes, while mica peels off into thin sheets. But some minerals are so similar that you have to use a high-powered microscope to tell them apart.

▲ This rock contains crystals of the blue mineral malachite. All minerals are crystalline. Sometimes they form large crystals that are easy to see, but some mineral crystals, like the malachite crystals here, are so small that they are only visible under a microscope (inset).

▶ Some minerals fluoresce, or glow, under ultraviolet light. The minerals shown here are zinc minerals from Franklin, New Jersey, USA. Miners used to use an ultraviolet light to find the areas rich in these minerals.

EARTH'S HISTORY BOOKS

Rocks are the Earth's history books. They tell us what a place was like millions of years ago. They show us what the weather was like, what animals and plants were alive, whether it was desert or swamp, land or sea, mountains or plains. Everything we know about the Earth's history comes from studying rocks.

A rock is a natural, solid piece of a planet, moon or asteroid. Most rocks are made of minerals, but some are made of dead plants and animals.

The three types of rock

Geologists group rocks into three categories: igneous, sedimentary and metamorphic. Each type forms in a different way.

▲ This pink granite is made of mineral crystals. These are pink feldspar, white feldspar, clear quartz and black mica.

Igneous rocks

Igneous rocks start out as hot liquid rock called *magma*. As the magma cools, mineral crystals begin to grow in it, and the liquid hardens. Sometimes magma turns solid underground. These rocks are called *plutonic*. Granite is a type of plutonic rock. Other times magma flows out on the surface before it turns solid. This kind of igneous rock is called *volcanic*. Basalt is the most common volcanic rock.

▲ Granite is an igneous rock that forms deep underground when hot, liquid rocks cool and harden.

▲ Sandstone is a sedimentary rock made of small grains of sand that settled out of water or air.

◄ Gneiss is a metamorphic rock. It began as a sedimentary rock, but after millions of years of being heated and squeezed, it turned into gneiss.

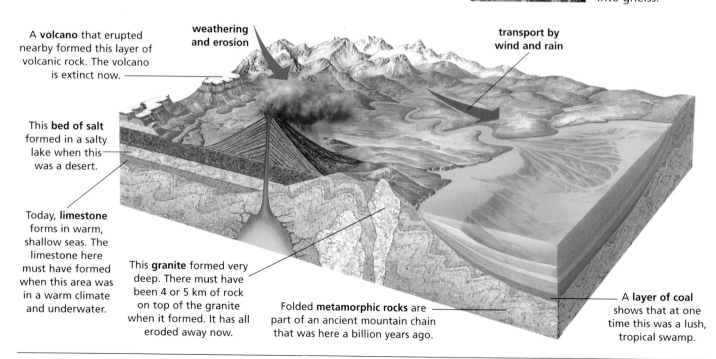

A **volcano** that erupted nearby formed this layer of volcanic rock. The volcano is extinct now.

weathering and erosion

transport by wind and rain

This **bed of salt** formed in a salty lake when this was a desert.

Today, **limestone** forms in warm, shallow seas. The limestone here must have formed when this area was in a warm climate and underwater.

This **granite** formed very deep. There must have been 4 or 5 km of rock on top of the granite when it formed. It has all eroded away now.

Folded **metamorphic rocks** are part of an ancient mountain chain that was here a billion years ago.

A **layer of coal** shows that at one time this was a lush, tropical swamp.

THE STORY OF A ROCK

Over millions of years rocks change or break down, and eventually become new rocks. This is called the *rock cycle*. Below is one example of a rock cycle.

1. Granite formed deep in the Earth's crust rises to the surface as the rocks above it slowly wear away.

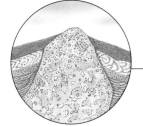

2. On the Earth's surface the solid granite is pelted with rain, frozen and thawed, cracked and broken by earthquakes, and pried apart by plants.

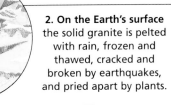

3. Pieces of granite are carried away by streams and rivers to the sea. The pieces slowly break up and wear down. Eventually they become sand and mud, mixed with pieces of other rocks on the beach.

6. The schist is buried deeper and gets even hotter. Parts of it get so hot that they melt. When the liquid cools, new granite may form.

5. As the rock is buried deeper, it gets hotter. The rock layers bend and fold. Over millions of years, new minerals grow from the sand and mud. A rock called schist forms.

4. Over time other rocks bury the muddy sand. The grains are squeezed together and cemented with minerals. The rock is now a muddy sandstone.

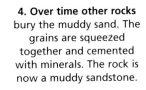

Sedimentary rocks

Loose pieces of rock such as pebbles, sand and mud are called sediments. Most sediments form when other rocks break down and erode (wear) away. Sediments are carried by rivers down to lakes or the sea, where they settle on the bottom. As more sediments settle on top of them, they are slowly squeezed together, eventually turning into sedimentary rocks. Sandstone is a sedimentary rock.

Some sedimentary rocks come from living things. Limestone is made of shells and skeletons of tiny sea creatures. Coal starts out as layers of dead swamp plants.

Metamorphic rocks

Metamorphic rocks are rocks that have been changed (*metamorphosed*) by heat and pressure. The heat and pressure can come in many ways. Heat from magma or hot igneous rocks can bake other rocks nearby. When rocks get buried, the weight of the rocks above squeezes them and the heat from inside the Earth cooks them. Rocks can also get squeezed when continents crash into each other.

Examples of metamorphic rocks include slate, which is metamorphosed shale, a sedimentary rock made from mud. Other examples include marble, which is metamorphosed limestone. Most metamorphic rocks take millions of years to form.

key words

- igneous rock
- metamorphic rock
- minerals
- sedimentary rock

◄ Though this rock was found on dry land, the ripple marks on it show that it formed in shallow water. Geologists can use rocks like these to work out what a place was like when the rock formed.

FOUR AND A HALF BILLION YEARS

Imagine that the entire 4.56 billion (4560 million) years of Earth history were squeezed into a single year. The Earth formed on 1 January. The Moon formed a few days later. Life began at the beginning of March, but large plants and animals didn't evolve until November. Dinosaurs lived only from 12 to 26 December. And human-like animals didn't evolve until 31 December at four o'clock in the afternoon.

Ever since geologists first began studying the Earth more than 200 years ago, they have been trying to unravel its history. By studying rocks and fossils, geologists can work out what was happening on Earth when the rocks formed. To work out when different events were taking place, they need to put the rocks and fossils in chronological order (oldest to youngest).

▶ This timeline shows how rocks can tell us about the Earth's history.

Chondrite meteorites are the oldest rocks in the Solar System. They formed over 4½ billion years ago, at the same time as the Sun and the planets.

This X-ray and drawing show a **fossil bacterium** from Australia that is about 3½ billion years old. It is one of the oldest fossils known on Earth.

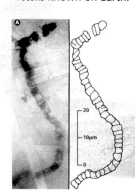

Evidence from rocks suggests that the Moon formed when a **small planet** smashed into the Earth soon after it was formed.

WHAT HAPPENED FIRST AT THE GRAND CANYON

The Grand Canyon in the western USA is one of the natural wonders of the world. Over millions of years, the Colorado River has cut through over 1500 m of rock, exposing layer after layer laid down over hundreds of millions of years. Using various basic principles (the laws of superposition and cross-cutting relationships, and the evidence of fossils; see main text), geologists can work out the order of events in the formation of the rocks.

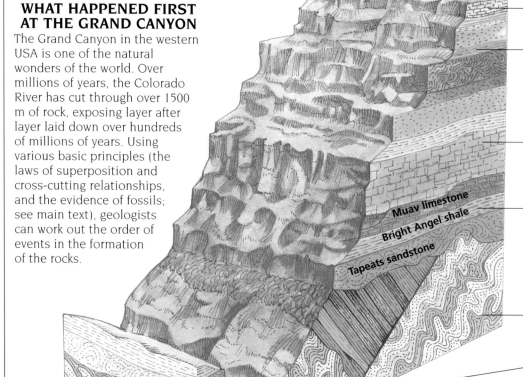

Muav limestone
Bright Angel shale
Tapeats sandstone

The Kaibab limestone is the youngest rock formation.

This uneven boundary is called an 'unconformity'. It marks a period of time where rocks were eroding away rather than forming.

The Redwall limestone must have formed after the Muav limestone and everything below it, but before everything above.

Fossils of trilobites in the Bright Angel shale and the Muav limestone show that the rocks must have formed in Cambrian or Devonian times, when trilobites were still alive on the Earth.

The Vishnu schist and gneiss is the oldest formation.

Granite cuts across the schist and gneiss, so it must be younger.

The Colorado River cuts through everything, so it must be youngest of all.

Trilobites were among the most successful early animals. This fossil is about 500 million years old.

Coal is a good fuel. It formed from the remains of forests that grew in the Carboniferous period, about 300 million years ago.

impact crater —

The **first land plant** fossils are about 420 million years old. The best-known of these is Cooksonia (shown).

An asteroid or comet hit central America 65 million years ago, making this huge **impact crater**. This event may have caused the extinction of the dinosaurs and other plants and animals.

These **human footprints** were made by our ancestors about 3.6 million years ago, as they walked through some soft volcanic ash in Tanzania.

Reading the rocks

Geologists can work out the sequence of events that created a rock formation by looking closely at rocks out in the field, making maps and studying fossils. There are three important things a geologist takes into account when trying to work out which rocks formed first.

The law of superposition

Sedimentary rocks (rocks formed by tiny fragments settling on the bottom of seas and lakes) and volcanic rocks (rocks made from the lava from volcanoes) form on top of each other. Therefore, the oldest rocks are at the bottom and the youngest are at the top. 'Superpose' means 'lie on top of'.

The law of cross-cutting relationships

Igneous rocks (rocks made from hot liquid rock) can form within cracks running through other rocks. A rock that cuts through or across another rock must be younger than the rock it cuts through.

Fossils

Over time, animals and plants have lived and then become extinct. They have left fossils in the sedimentary rocks that were forming when they died. Using the law of superposition (older fossils lie beneath younger fossils), geologists have been able to put ancient plants and animals in chronological order.

If you know when a particular species (or a group of species) was alive, then you can use its fossils as a time-marker. For instance, if a sedimentary rock has dinosaur bones in it, it must have formed during the Mesozoic era when dinosaurs were alive. Fossils can also help you work out whether a rock in one part of the world formed before, after, or at about the same time as a rock in another part of the world.

Working out how old rocks are relative to each other is called relative dating.

Dating rocks using radioactivity

One way geologists work out the absolute age of a rock in years is by studying the atoms in a mineral grain in the rock. Every mineral is composed of atoms. Some kinds of atoms turn into different atoms over time. For instance, some uranium turns into lead, and some potassium turns into argon. These atoms are 'radioactive' because they give off radiation as they change.

If you know how fast the 'parent' atoms turn into 'daughter' atoms, and you measure how many parent atoms and daughter atoms there are in the mineral grains, you can calculate the age of the rock. This is known as radiometric dating.

key words

- absolute age
- Earth history
- geological time
- radiometric dating
- relative dating

ANCIENT REMAINS

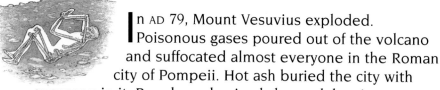

In AD 79, Mount Vesuvius exploded. Poisonous gases poured out of the volcano and suffocated almost everyone in the Roman city of Pompeii. Hot ash buried the city with everyone in it. People and animals burned, leaving imprints of their bodies in the ash. In just hours, thousands of people became fossils preserved in rock.

Fossils are remains of living things, preserved in rocks. There are many kinds of fossil. Some, like mammoth bones or shells in limestone, are actual pieces of things that were once alive. Others, such as leaf imprints or dinosaur tracks are signs of a plant or animal that was once alive.

Fossilization

Most things don't turn into fossils as quickly as the people in Pompeii. It usually takes thousands or millions of years.

When something dies and its body sits out in the air and rain, it will decompose. Eventually there won't be much sign of it anywhere. But if the body or the tracks are quickly buried by sediments (such as mud or sand) then they can be preserved. As the sediments turn into rock, the fossil is locked in.

Fossils tell a story

Fossils are the only evidence we have for what life was like on Earth in prehistoric

▶ How a sea creature becomes a fossil.

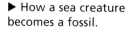 key words
- evolution
- fossil
- fossilization
- sediment

▼ The fossil of an ammonite, nearly 200 million years old. Ammonites were shelled sea creatures that became extinct 65 million years ago, at the same time as the dinosaurs.

times. They tell us what animals and plants were alive and what the environment was like at different times in the Earth's history.

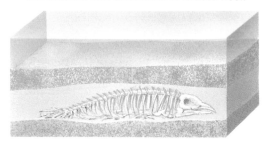
The creature dies and settles to the sea floor.

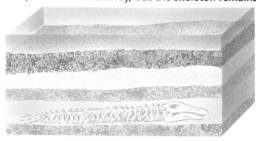
Over time it gets covered by sediments (mud and sand). The flesh rots away, but the **skeleton remains.**

As the sediments pile up, they harden to form **rock.** The skeleton gets squashed and broken.

Earth movements lift up the rock layers, and the sea level drops.

The rocks are exposed to the weather and the upper layers are slowly worn away, revealing the **fossilized skeleton.**

OUR JIGSAW PLANET

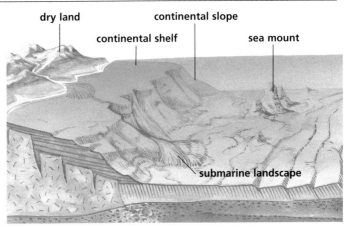

dry land

continental shelf

continental slope

sea mount

submarine landscape

When the dinosaurs first roamed the land 230 million years ago, there was only one huge continent on Earth. This supercontinent is known as Pangaea, which means 'all land'. About 200 million years ago, Pangaea started to break apart into the continents we know today.

Continents are the dry, high land that most people live on. If the entire crust of the Earth were all the same – the same rock, the same thickness, the same age – everything would be underwater. The reason continents are high and dry and ocean floors are low and underwater is because they are made of different rocks.

Floating rock

Continental crust is very thick and the rocks are relatively light. The ocean crust, however, is thinner and denser. The continents float high on the mantle, while the ocean crust sinks low in the same way that a tall, light, empty ship floats higher on the sea than a short, heavy one.

ALFRED WEGENER

In 1912, a German scientist called Alfred Wegener (1880–1930) suggested that the continents drift around on Earth's surface.

Wegener had many reasons for believing this was true. He had noticed that if you took away the Atlantic Ocean, South America and Africa would fit neatly together. On an island in the Arctic, he had found rocks that could only have formed near the Equator. The Equator couldn't move, so the island must have moved. Wegener also noticed that there were fossils of the same extinct animals and plants on different continents. Surely these creatures didn't swim across the oceans? It made more sense if all the continents had been together at one time and then split apart.

▲ This diagram shows the edge of a continent. Continents seem smaller than they actually are because the edge of the continent (the continental shelf) is covered by shallow seas.

◀ These folded rocks in Hamersley Gorge, Western Australia, are some of the oldest on Earth. They are part of an ancient section of a continent (a craton) that is more than 3½ billion years old.

⬤ key words
- continent
- continental drift
- continental shelf and slope
- fault
- plate
- plate tectonics

EARTH'S PLATES

Earth's surface is broken into about a dozen plates. Some plates are made of continental and ocean crust, and others are just ocean crust. At the edges of the plates are faults where the rocks are broken and the plates move against each another. Earthquakes occur along the plate boundaries all the time. Since it's not always easy to see the faults that separate the plates, geologists use earthquakes to find the boundaries instead.

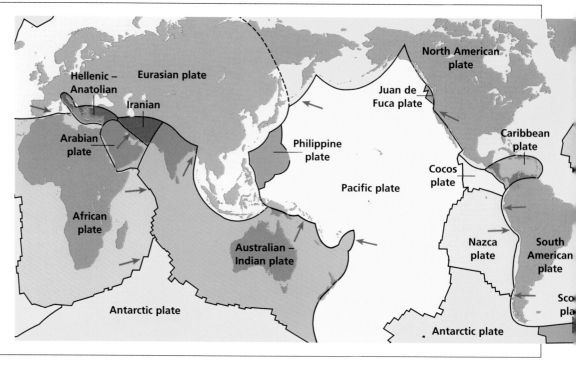

Hellenic – Anatolian
Eurasian plate
North American plate
Iranian
Juan de Fuca plate
Arabian plate
Philippine plate
Caribbean plate
Cocos plate
Pacific plate
African plate
Nazca plate
South American plate
Australian – Indian plate
Antarctic plate
Sco pla
Antarctic plate

▲ Triassic period

colliding plates

shape of today's continents

▼ late Cretaceous period

ATLANTIC OCEAN

▲▶ These maps show how the face of the Earth has changed in the last 240 million years. The continents formed Pangaea in the late Triassic period, 237 million years ago. By the late Cretaceous, about 94 million years ago, the Atlantic Ocean had begun to open as Pangaea split up. By the end of the last Ice Age (about 18,000 years ago) the continents were almost in their present positions.

In a few places, the ocean crust is so thick that it does rise out of the sea. It forms ocean islands like Hawaii and Iceland. Even though they are dry land, the islands are not continents.

Continental rocks

The continents are made of rocks of all ages and all kinds – igneous, sedimentary and metamorphic. Continents probably began forming soon after the Earth formed 4.5 billion years ago. But because rocks wear down and get buried and melted, it is unlikely that any of the first rocks still survive. The oldest rock we know of is a 4 billion-year-old metamorphic rock from Canada.

▼ last Ice Age

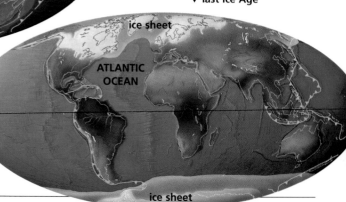

ice sheet
ATLANTIC OCEAN
ice sheet

Plates

When people talk about 'continental drift' today, what they usually mean is 'plate tectonics'. Alfred Wegener was right that the continents move around on the Earth's surface, but it is not only the continents that move. The sea floor moves too.

The Earth's surface is like a jigsaw puzzle, broken into many pieces. Geologists call these jigsaw pieces *plates* and they are made up of both continents and ocean floors. The plates move around like icebergs packed together on a frozen lake. They ram into each other, grate past each other, ride on top of one another, and try to move away from each other.

Plates don't stay the same forever. They grow and shrink. Sometimes they rip into two or three new plates. At other times they collide with another plate to form a new, bigger plate.

The theory of plate tectonics

The word *tectonics* refers to the forces that create large features such as mountains, volcanoes and continents on the Earth's surface. For instance, *bulldozer tectonics* would be the theory that huge bulldozers push everything into place. *Plate tectonics* is the theory geologists prefer. It says that huge slabs of crust and mantle move around on the Earth's surface, causing earthquakes, making volcanoes erupt, and creating continents, ocean floors, tall mountains and deep valleys.

How plates move

No one is exactly sure what makes the plates move. Most geologists think that they are carried around by currents in the mantle below.

Even though the mantle is solid rock, it can flow. It flows because it is hotter in some places and cooler in others. In the same way that hot air rises and cold air sinks, hot rocks rise and cold rocks sink. The rocks near the Earth's core are so hot that they rise up towards the surface. At the same time, the cool rocks near the crust sink. The mantle flows very slowly, just several centimetres every year.

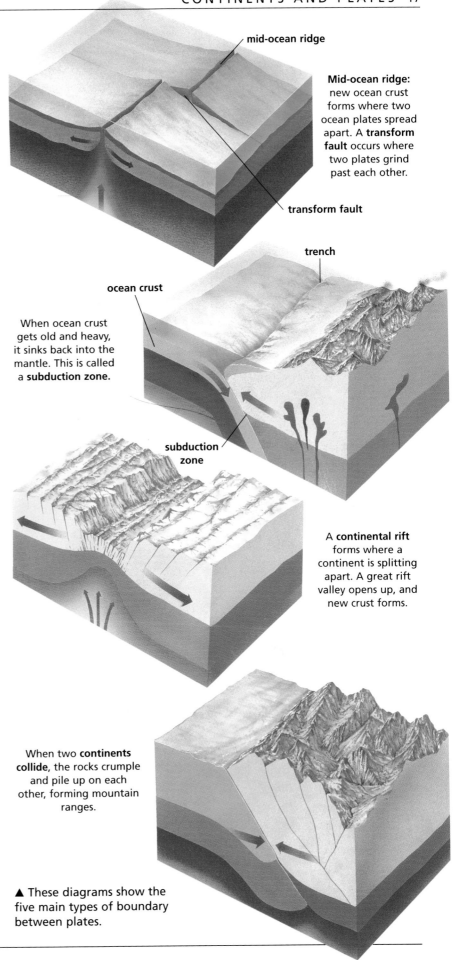

Mid-ocean ridge: new ocean crust forms where two ocean plates spread apart. A **transform fault** occurs where two plates grind past each other.

When ocean crust gets old and heavy, it sinks back into the mantle. This is called a **subduction zone**.

A **continental rift** forms where a continent is splitting apart. A great rift valley opens up, and new crust forms.

When two **continents collide,** the rocks crumple and pile up on each other, forming mountain ranges.

▲ These diagrams show the five main types of boundary between plates.

ROCKY PEAKS

Eighty million years ago, India was an island continent 5000 kilometres south of mainland Asia. Then India and the sea floor round it began slowly drifting northwards. The floor of the Indian Ocean dived beneath Tibet, and volcanoes erupted.

Eventually, the Indian continent crashed into mainland Asia, squeezing and breaking the rocks and folding them into contorted shapes. As the rocks piled on top of each other, the continent got thicker. Rocks that had formed on the bottom of the sea were thrust upwards and became part of the highest mountain range on Earth – the Himalayas.

How mountains form

There are two main kinds of mountain ranges: volcanic mountains, and fold and thrust mountains. Both kinds form over millions of years as the broken pieces of Earth's surface (the tectonic plates) collide with each other.

Volcanic mountain ranges, like the Cascades in the USA and the Andes in South America, form where the ocean floor dives beneath the edge of a continent. The rocks beneath the continent melt and then erupt as lava and ash. Over millions of

▶ The Torres del Paine mountains in Chile are part of the Andes mountain chain. The peaks are made of granite, which formed deep underground. The granite slowly came to the surface as the rocks above it eroded away. Glaciers have carved the rock into sharp peaks.

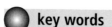 **key words**
- folds
- Himalayas
- mountains
- tectonic plates

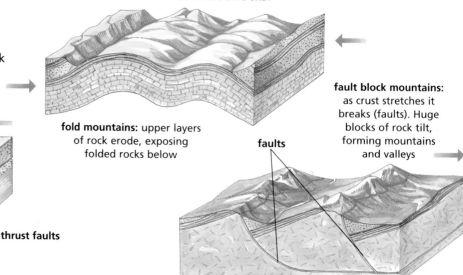

years, the volcanoes grow to form long, tall mountain chains.

Fold and thrust mountains, like the Himalayas in Asia and the Appalachians in the USA, form when two land masses crash into one another. As they collide, the rocks crumple and get pushed up into mountain ranges.

Shaping mountains

Once mountains begin to form, they are shaped by other forces such as running water, glacier ice and gravity. At one time, the Highlands of Scotland were as tall and jagged as the Alps. But as they got older, they wore down. Many ancient mountain ranges are now just low hills or flat plains of folded rocks.

▼ Thrust mountains and fold mountains form when two continents collide. Fault block mountains form when a continent has been stretched.

fold mountains: upper layers of rock erode, exposing folded rocks below

fault block mountains: as crust stretches it breaks (faults). Huge blocks of rock tilt, forming mountains and valleys

faults

thrust faults

thrust mountains: layers of rock thrust on top of each other as continents collide

WHEN THE EARTH CRACKS

In the early morning of 17 August 1999, rocks began to break deep beneath the small city of Izmit, Turkey. As they broke, they moved past each other. Izmit and the surrounding area shook. By the end of the earthquake, there was a tear in the ground more than 100 kilometres long, and the rocks had moved 3 metres.

The earthquake at Izmit destroyed hundreds of buildings and killed 18,000 people. It also created a tsunami, a huge sea wave that drowned part of the Turkish coastline. Earthquakes happen when rocks break and then move along large cracks, called faults, in the Earth's crust.

Breaking rocks

The surface of the Earth is made of many large pieces, or *plates*, that are moving very slowly. Most earthquakes occur at the edges of these plates, where they grate against one another. In some places, the rocks are moving all the time, so small tremors happen almost every day. In other places, the rocks try to move past one another, but they get stuck. The stress builds up for many years until finally the rock snaps and a powerful earthquake jolts the land.

▶ Aerial view of the San Andreas fault in California, the site of many earthquakes. The city of San Francisco lies directly on the fault, and suffered major earthquakes in 1906, 1989 and 1994.

 key words

- earthquake
- fault
- plate
- seismology

Key
earthquake depths:
- less than 70 km
- 70 to 300 km
- 300 to 700 km

▼ A seismogram of the Izmit earthquake. Seismograms are recordings of how the ground shakes. Even though earthquakes only destroy things in the small area near where the rocks move, seismic waves pass all the way through and around the Earth. This seismogram was recorded in Urumquin in West China, thousands of kilometres away from Izmit.

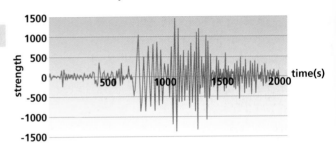

Seismic waves

When rocks break, they release energy into the other rocks nearby. The energy is called *seismic energy* and it travels through the Earth as *seismic waves*. Seismic waves travel through rock in almost the same way that ocean waves travel through water. Some travel through the inside of the Earth and others travel around the Earth on the surface. Some move the rocks up and down and some move them from side to side. Some squeeze and stretch the rock. Seismic waves are what shake the ground and the buildings during an earthquake.

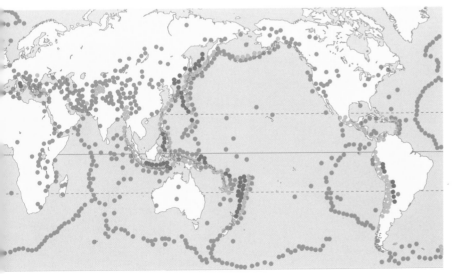

◀ A map of strong earthquakes that occurred between 1977 and 1992 shows that earthquakes are concentrated in particular areas. They also occur at different depths. Deep earthquakes occur near ocean trenches, where the ocean crust dives into the mantle below it.

MOUNTAINS OF FIRE

I n June 1991, Mount Pinatubo, a volcano in the Philippines, erupted. Ash blasted high into the sky, and flows of lava, steam and rubble came pouring down the mountain. Houses were crushed by the ash, and anyone caught in a flow was instantly killed.

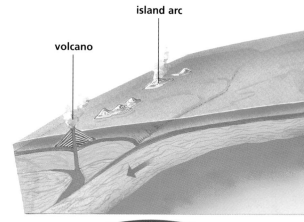

No one had ever seen Pinatubo erupt before, but geologists knew it was ready. For two months it had been warning people with earthquakes and belches of steam and gas. Pinatubo exploded with such power that it blasted 200 metres off its top and created a huge *crater* (deep, steep-sided hollow) at its summit.

▶ Lava can be hotter than 1200 °C, so hot that it glows. This is a 'fire fountain' of lava photographed during an eruption in Costa Rica in 1991.

What is a volcano?

Volcanoes are places where *lava* (molten rock) erupts onto the surface of the Earth. There are many types of volcano.

Stratovolcanoes are large, steep volcanoes made of layers of lava and ash. They are so steep because the lava is so thick and sticky that it can't flow very far before it

▼ An erupting stratovolcano, showing what a volcano looks like on the inside as well as the outside.

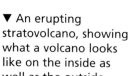

hardens. It piles up close to the *vent* (opening at the top), creating a cone-like shape. Large stratovolcanoes grow from many eruptions over hundreds of thousands or even millions of years.

Shield volcanoes are broad with gentle slopes. These volcanoes are made of layer after layer of hot, runny lava that flows a long way before it turns solid.

Other types of volcano include long fissures where lava erupts quietly for years on end, and huge holes in the ground called calderas. The size and shape of each volcano depends on what it is made of and how it has erupted in the past.

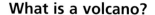

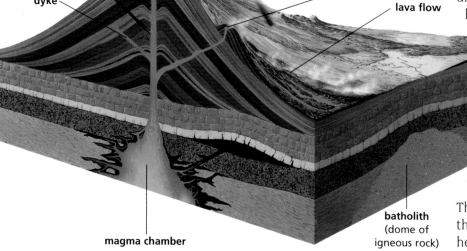

main vent

cone of ash, rock and lava

dyke

magma chamber

cloud of ash and steam

volcanic bomb

side vent

lava flow

batholith (dome of igneous rock)

Why do volcanoes erupt?

The inside of the Earth is very hot. Some of the heat escapes through volcanoes, which helps the Earth to cool down.

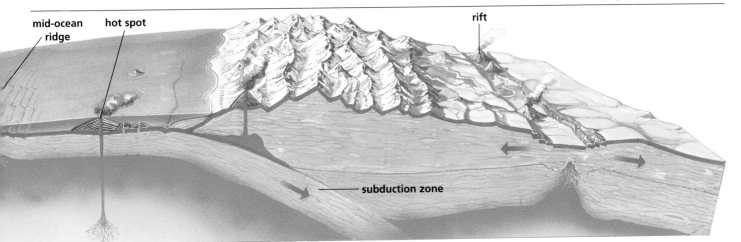

mid-ocean ridge | hot spot | rift | subduction zone

Deep underground, in the Earth's mantle and crust, there are places where the rocks melt. When they melt, they form *magma* – a hot slush of mineral crystals, liquid rock and gas. Magma is not as dense as the rock around it, so it begins to rise upwards through cracks. A lot of the magma never makes it to the surface and it hardens underground. But some of it forces its way through openings or weak spots in the ground, and erupts. As soon as magma erupts, it is called lava.

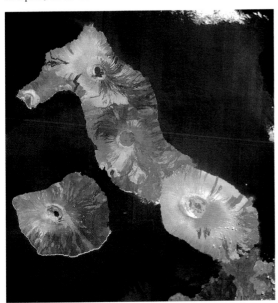

▲ Isabella Island in the Galapagos is made up of a number of shield volcanoes. This image was taken by a satellite.

Types of eruption

Eruptions at shield volcanoes are usually very calm. The lava pours gently out onto the ground. Eruptions at stratovolcanoes like Pinatubo are usually explosive. The way a volcano erupts depends how thick and sticky the magma is, and on how much gas the magma contains.

When magma forms, it is under pressure from the weight of the rocks above. As it moves up through these rocks, there is less weight above and the pressure decreases. The gas in the magma expands and forms bubbles – like when you unscrew the top of a fizzy drink.

If the magma is thin and runny, then the gas bubbles can move easily through it and out to the surface. The magma flows easily and it erupts calmly. But if the magma is thick and sticky, the bubbles can't escape. Instead they explode, shattering the magma into small pieces and throwing them out of the volcano and high up into the air. This ash rains down on the volcano and the surrounding area. The explosions can also cause searing hot flows of lava, steam and rock to come racing out of the volcano at 100 kilometres per hour.

▼ Most of the world's active volcanoes are around the edge of the Pacific Ocean, an area known as the 'Ring of Fire'.

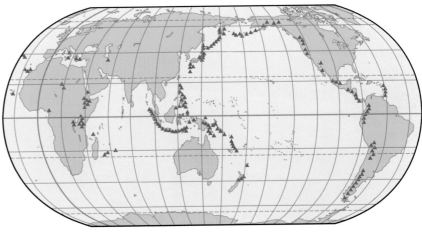

▲ Different types of volcano form in different places. Explosive stratovolcanoes form near ocean trenches, where a section of the Earth's crust is diving beneath another. Some shield volcanoes form where the ocean crust is being torn apart. Large shield volcanoes form over 'hot spots', where a lot of magma is forming in the mantle.

key words

- caldera
- crater
- lava
- magma
- vent
- volcano

NATURAL SCULPTORS

In northern Venezuela in December 1999, nearly a metre of rain fell in just three days. The rain soaked into the El Avila Mountains until the rocks and soil were so wet that parts of the mountain began to slide down towards the sea. Tonnes of mud, rocks, and boulders the size of houses came roaring down the valleys, cutting through the mountainside, burying villages, and creating new landforms at the base of the mountains.

▲ Mud and silt washed from the hills cover the streets of Caracas, Venezuela, after floods in 1999.

The El Avila landslide is a dramatic example of *erosion*. Erosion is when rocks fall apart and then move from one place to another. Landslides can move tonnes of rock in just seconds. The strong waves and winds in hurricanes can erode a beach overnight. But most erosion happens slowly, over thousands or millions of years.

key words

- erosion
- weathering

Weakening the rocks

Before erosion can take place, rocks have to be weakened. Rocks are constantly falling apart. When rocks are exposed to air and water, the minerals in them start to change or break up. For example, iron minerals get rusty, while hard feldspars turn into soft clay, and salt dissolves completely. This process is called *weathering*. Weathering turns solid rock into soft soil.

Weathering happens more quickly in warm, wet areas than in cold, dry regions.

▼ Uluru, also called Ayer's Rock, is a monolith ('single rock') that rises 350 m above the Australian desert. It is made of a hard rock. At one time, the whole of the desert was at the same level. But weathering and erosion gradually wore away the softer rock around Uluru, leaving it rising above the plain.

Some rocks weather much more easily than others. Salt, for instance, quickly dissolves away in water. Granite, however, takes much longer to weather away.

What causes weathering?

Air and water cause most weathering. Sometimes they change the chemicals in the rocks, and sometimes they just break apart the rock physically. When water freezes, it expands. If it seeps into a crack in a rock and then freezes, it can pry the rock apart. Wind can pick up small rock particles and hurl them at other rocks. Many rocks in deserts get sand-blasted in this way by the wind.

Living things can also weather rocks. For example, plants growing in cracks slowly pry the rocks apart with their roots. People also cause weathering by walking and driving on rocks. People also pollute the atmosphere, causing acid rain, which eats away at rocks.

mesa

mountain peak

ice and snow

waterfall

screes landscape

gorge

flood plain

estuary

stack

cliffs

natural arch

How erosion happens

Once rocks have weathered, it is much easier for them to erode.

Many things can cause erosion, but water is the most powerful force. Rain washes soil into rivers. Rivers scour the land, breaking rocks and then taking them downstream towards the ocean. Glaciers (rivers of ice) grind up the rocks beneath and beside them, and then dump ground-up rock at the end of the glacier.

Wind is important because it creates waves that pound the seashore, breaking down cliffs and moving sand from one place to another. Earthquakes can speed up erosion by breaking and crushing rocks. More importantly, they can trigger huge landslides, and cause tsunamis – giant waves that erode coasts.

All of these forces are helped along by gravity. If a rock is weathered enough, and the slopes are steep enough, gravity alone will be enough to cause erosion.

Creating new landforms

Weathering and erosion shape the Earth's landscape. Running water cuts river valleys and etches out caves. Waves shape the shoreline. Glaciers carve mountains into sharp peaks. Every piece of rock that gets eroded from one place, gets deposited in another. Erosion is one of nature's ways of rearranging the landscape.

▲ This diagram shows a few of the many landforms on Earth that have been shaped by erosion – the forces of water, wind and gravity.

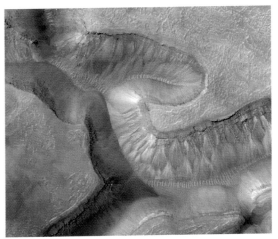

◄ The canyon in this photo of Mars looks as if it was carved by running water. There is no water on the surface of Mars today. Landforms like these show that there was probably water eroding Mars's surface millions of years ago.

UNDERGROUND CAVERNS

In a limestone cave, deep in a mountainside, thousands of icicle-shaped stalactites hang from the ceiling, and tall, pointed stalagmites jut up from the floor. Water drips slowly down the wall, trickling over paintings made by prehistoric people. A caver looking for new passageways disturbs thousands of bats asleep on the ceiling. The underground river that runs through the cave is slowly eating through the rock, making the cave bigger every day.

Caves are natural underground rooms and passageways. Some are small, but others have huge chambers the size of cathedrals, and passages that extend for many kilometres.

Different kinds of cave

There are several kinds of cave. Sea caves form where waves pound a cliff and slowly carve a hole in the weak rocks. Ice caves are caverns in glaciers, carved out by rivers. Lava tube caves form near volcanoes. As a river of lava flows, its surface cools and turns solid, but the lava inside stays warm and keeps flowing. Eventually the liquid lava drains away, leaving an empty cave.

 key words

- cave
- sinkhole
- stalactite
- stalagmite

▼ How a limestone cave forms. Acidic rainwater seeps through cracks in the limestone and slowly dissolves away the rock.

▲ These 200-metre limestone pinnacles near Guilin, China, are all that is left of a thick bed of limestone. Over millions of years, water has dissolved away the rest of the rock. There are small passages and caves within the pinnacles.

Limestone caves

The most common kinds of cave are limestone caves. Limestone is a rock made of the mineral calcite, which is a calcium compound. Caves form when slightly acidic water seeps through cracks in the rock and dissolves it away. Similar caves can form in other rocks – such as marble, gypsum and dolomite – that dissolve in acidic water.

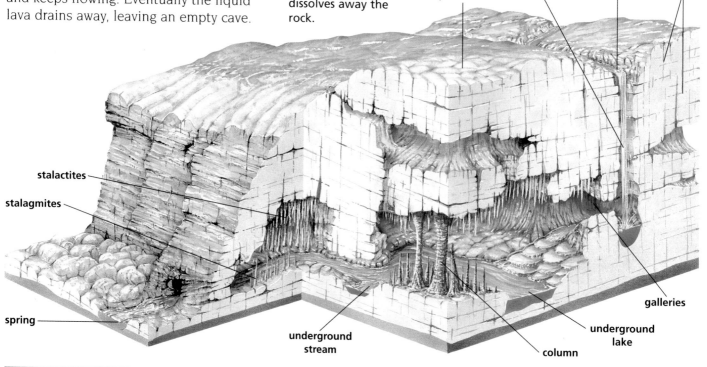

limestone pavement · chimney · sinkhole · joints

stalactites · stalagmites · spring · underground stream · column · underground lake · galleries

DRY AS A BONE

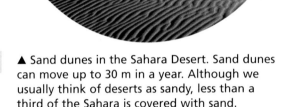

The Rub'al Khali desert of Saudi Arabia is the largest sand sea on Earth. Giant sand dunes shaped like stars, crescents and fishhooks grow up to 150 metres high. It only rains about 15 centimetres each year and some years it doesn't rain at all. There are not enough plants to hold down the sand or block the winds, so the dunes are continuously changing shape as they drift over the hard rock below.

A desert is a place where very little rain or snow falls. The rain that does fall evaporates quickly in the dry air. Some deserts are hot and some are cold. Some are sandy and some are rocky. The one thing they all have in common is that they are dry.

No rain

There are several reasons why rainfall is low in some parts of the world. Rain comes from clouds, and most of the water in clouds comes from water that evaporated from the oceans. Deserts like the Gobi in the middle of Asia are dry because they are so far from the oceans. By the time the air gets to the Gobi Desert, it has lost most of its moisture.

The desert in Argentina is dry because it

key words

- desert
- rain
- rain shadow
- winds

The driest deserts on Earth are the cold, dry valleys of Antarctica.

▼ A desert landscape, similar to one you might see in the American South-west.

▲ Sand dunes in the Sahara Desert. Sand dunes can move up to 30 m in a year. Although we usually think of deserts as sandy, less than a third of the Sahara is covered with sand.

is on the 'rain shadow' side of the Andes Mountains. When moist air from the Pacific Ocean reaches the mountains, it rises up. As it rises it cools, and all the moisture falls as rain on the ocean side of the mountains.

The largest deserts, like the Sahara, the Rub'al Khali and the Great Australian, are in the subtropics, just north and south of the tropical region around the Equator. The subtropics are so dry because the air comes from the tropics, where it has already lost most of its water.

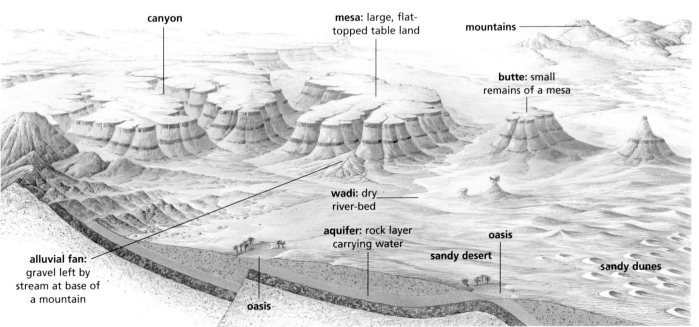

canyon

mesa: large, flat-topped table land

mountains

butte: small remains of a mesa

wadi: dry river-bed

aquifer: rock layer carrying water

oasis

sandy desert

sandy dunes

alluvial fan: gravel left by stream at base of a mountain

oasis

FRESH WATER

In a remote region of southern Siberia lies the deepest lake on Earth, Lake Baykal. Baykal is 630 kilometres long and over 1500 metres deep. It holds more fresh water than any other lake or river on Earth.

valleys, and deposit (drop) mud, sand and gravel in others. The river channel can move back and forth across a valley, becoming more winding or straightening out. If there is a lot of rain upstream, the river will cut a wider channel or flood the banks. Once in a while, usually during a flood, part of a river will jump over to a completely new course. How fast a river changes depends on how much water is flowing, how fast it is flowing, and what kind of rock it is flowing over.

The other main sources of Earth's fresh water are rain and snow, groundwater (water in the rocks and underground), and rivers and streams.

Rivers and streams

When rain falls on land, it runs over the ground or through the soil and gathers with other rainwater in low areas, where it forms streams. Small streams join to make larger streams, and then eventually come together to form rivers. The rivers run until they empty into the sea or a lake.

There are many large rivers on Earth, and endless numbers of smaller rivers (tributaries) that feed them. Even in deserts there are dry stream-beds (called wadis or arroyos) that drain water off the desert when it rains.

Changing courses

Rivers are always changing. They not only change themselves, but also shape the land around them. They scour out an ever-deeper channel in some places, making

▶ Rivers can take different forms, and they vary along their course from the mountains to the sea. This illustration shows a meandering river.

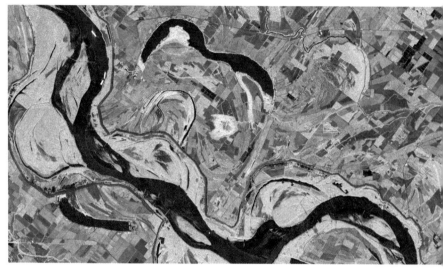

▲ A satellite image of the Mississippi River in the USA. It is a meandering river, which changes its course as it erodes its banks on one side, and deposits mud on the other. You can see signs of old river channels in the fields on either side of its current course.

Lakes

If water gathers in a hollow and doesn't quickly evaporate, sink into the ground, or run off in a stream, a lake forms. The hollows in which lakes form can be made in different ways.

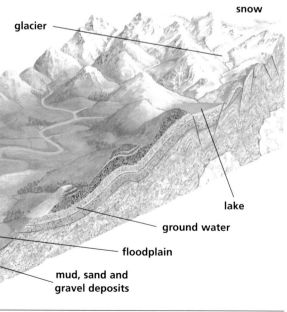

rain and snow

glacier

meanders

oxbow lake

delta

ocean

lake

ground water

floodplain

mud, sand and gravel deposits

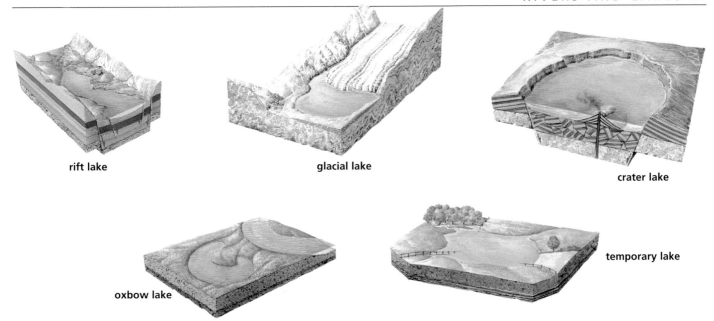

rift lake

glacial lake

crater lake

oxbow lake

temporary lake

Glacial lakes

The most common kind of lake is a glacial lake. Glacial lakes such as those in the Lake District of England or the Great Lakes area of North America fill depressions that glaciers scoured out of the land thousands of years ago.

Rift-valley lakes

Long, deep lakes such as Lake Baykal and Lake Tanganyika in eastern Africa fill rift valleys. Rift valleys form when a continent starts to rip apart. The continental crust (the surface layer of the Earth) stretches and breaks. Then blocks of the crust drop down to form a depression.

Crater lakes

Crater Lake in Oregon, USA, fills a volcanic caldera. When volcanoes erupt, lava erupts out of the ground, leaving an empty chamber below. The land drops down to fill the chasm, forming a large crater called a caldera, which can then fill with water. Small crater lakes can form at the tops of volcanoes that have blown their tops off. Lakes also fill impact craters, where meteorites have hit the Earth and exploded, creating a hole in the ground.

Temporary lakes

Just as there are temporary rivers on Earth, there are temporary lakes. The Lake Eyre Basin is a huge low area in the desert of

▲ Different types of lake. Lakes form in low areas where water collects.

There are more than 70 lakes beneath the ice sheets in Antarctica. The largest one, Lake Vostok, is 230 km long and 50 km across. It lies 4 km beneath the ice.

 key words

- delta
- groundwater
- lakes
- rift
- rivers
- streams
- tributary

▶ Glacial lakes fill depressions (low areas) that were scoured out by glaciers that moved across the land during the last Ice Age.

Australia. Lake Eyre fills with water only once every 10 or 20 years when it rains hard for a few days. It then dries up within a few weeks. Lakes that come and go with the rains are known as playa lakes.

Groundwater

There is about 70 times more water in the ground than in all the lakes, rivers and streams on Earth combined. Groundwater is water that seeps into the ground and then collects in the spaces between grains in rock such as sandstone. It flows through the rock, in some cases for millions of years, before coming back out of the ground as a spring. Even in the driest parts of the world, where there are no permanent rivers or lakes, there is groundwater.

RIVERS OF ICE

Almost the entire continent of Antarctica is covered in ice. Two huge ice sheets, up to 3 kilometres thick, flow very slowly from the centre of the continent out towards the sea. As the ice flows, it grinds up the rocks below, carries pieces to the ocean, and dumps them in. As the ice sheet melts, huge chunks break off into icebergs that float out to sea.

Ice sheets (also called ice caps) and glaciers are thick masses of ice that flow over land.

Rock made of ice

If snow falls in the winter, but doesn't completely melt during the summer, it gradually piles up. As it piles up, the snow gets packed tighter and tighter. Just as loose sediments turn into solid rock, so loose snow turns into solid ice. Eventually, the pile of ice and snow gets so thick that it starts to flow. A glacier has formed.

Glaciers and ice caps can form anywhere that it is cold and snowy, from the high mountains near the Equator to low elevations near the Poles. They can be as small as a few hundred metres across, or as large as a continent.

▶ This satellite photo over Antarctica shows Byrd Glacier (right) and a smaller glacier (top left) flowing from the coast into the permanently frozen Ross Ice Shelf (top).

key words

- crevasse
- glacier
- ice cap and ice sheet
- moraine

Flowing rock

Gravity makes glaciers flow. Inside the glacier, the ice crystals change shape and slide past each other. Glaciers in the mountains flow downhill, whereas huge ice sheets spread outwards under their own weight. In relatively warm areas, there is a lot of water in the glacier. It collects at the base, and then acts like grease so the glacier can slide down the mountain. Warm glaciers can move a few metres every day. Polar glaciers, however, are so cold that they are frozen to the rock beneath them. They move much more slowly, just a few centimetres each day.

▼ Glaciers play a big part in shaping many landscapes. As the glacier moves, the ice scrapes away the rock beneath it and on either side. High up on the mountain the glacier carves cirques (hollows) between mountain ridges, while lower down it gouges out U-shaped valleys. The crushed rock is pushed out at the sides and snout of the glacier as moraines (big piles of stones and boulders) or deposits of even smaller rock particles.

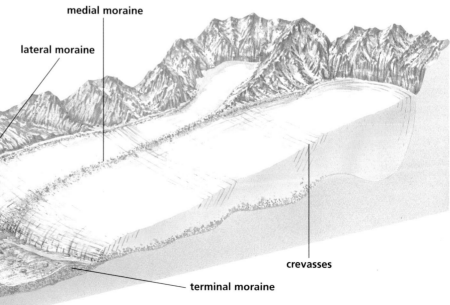

medial moraine
lateral moraine
drumlin
stream
crevasses
terminal moraine

WHERE LAND MEETS SEA

Some coasts are sandy, with soft, wide beaches. Some are muddy deltas at the mouth of a river. Other coasts are lined with boulders and pebbles. Some are straight and some are jagged, with hundreds of bays and inlets. In some places the land slopes gradually towards the ocean for hundreds of kilometres, and in others it drops off suddenly into the sea with a steep cliff.

A coast is where the land meets the sea. Coasts are constantly changing.

Building and destroying coasts

A map of a shoreline today might look very different from a map made a hundred years ago. This is because coastlines change over time.

Rivers bring sediments to the sea, and their deltas grow. The ocean erodes rocks from one part of the coast and then moves them to another. Cliffs retreat inland as waves hammer away at the rocks. Over millions of years, a hilly coast with cliffs and boulders can evolve into a wide, gently sloping sandy plain.

Sinking and rising

Some coasts are actually sinking into the sea or rising up out of it. In the last ice age glaciers covered northern Britain, pushing down the land under their weight. Since the ice melted around 10,000 years ago this land has been rising up, slowly tilting the south coast of Britain into the sea.

The coasts of California, Japan and the Mediterranean have recently been pushed up out of the ocean during powerful earthquakes. Coasts also change as sea levels rise and fall.

 key words
- beach
- coast
- erosion
- shore

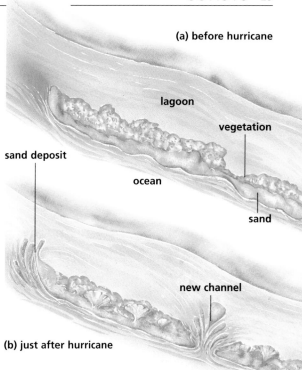

(a) before hurricane

lagoon

vegetation

sand deposit

ocean

sand

new channel

(b) just after hurricane

▲ Barrier islands are strips of loose sand that protect the mainland from the ocean. They change shape all the time as they are easily moved by wind and water. A hurricane can change a barrier island in less than a day.

▼ The shape of a coastline depends on things like how strong the waves and currents are, how much sand and mud is being carried by the ocean water, how the rocks along the coast respond to being battered by the waves, and how the landscape was shaped in the past.

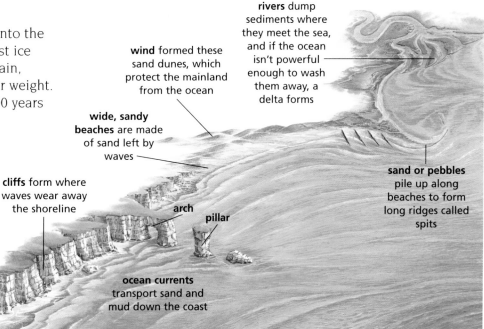

rivers dump sediments where they meet the sea, and if the ocean isn't powerful enough to wash them away, a delta forms

wind formed these sand dunes, which protect the mainland from the ocean

wide, sandy beaches are made of sand left by waves

cliffs form where waves wear away the shoreline

arch

pillar

sand or pebbles pile up along beaches to form long ridges called spits

ocean currents transport sand and mud down the coast

A BILLION BILLION TONNES OF WATER

Giant worms, blind shrimps, beds of clams and webs of primitive bacteria grow around springs of scalding hot water jetting out of the sea floor. These hot springs contain minerals that feed the animals and form strange pinnacles of rock. This is the scene on some parts of the ocean floor, 3 kilometres below the surface.

The world ocean is made up of all five oceans on Earth – the Atlantic, Pacific, Indian, Arctic and Southern oceans. Altogether, they cover almost three-quarters of Earth's surface.

Salt water

There are a billion billion tonnes of salt water in the ocean. Ocean water is salty because it is full of minerals dissolved in it. Some of the minerals are brought from the continents by rivers and winds. Others come from the hot springs at the bottom of the ocean. If the entire ocean evaporated, it would leave a layer of salt 50 metres thick. Much of this salt would be sodium chloride – common table salt.

key words
- current
- ocean
- water

▼ Waves are caused by the wind. The size of waves depends on how strongly and for how long the wind has been blowing. Waves over 30 m high have been recorded.

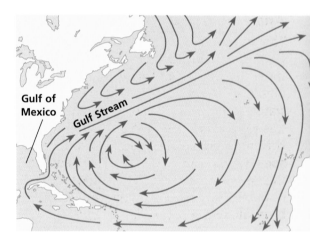

▶ The Gulf Stream is a current of warm surface water that flows from the Gulf of Mexico north-east towards Europe.

Gulf of Mexico

Gulf Stream

Currents

Ocean water flows around the Earth in great rivers called currents. Currents on the ocean's surface are driven by the winds. They travel in more or less the same direction that the wind most commonly blows.

There are also currents that flow from the surface towards the sea floor and down along the ocean bottom. These currents flow because parts of the oceans are colder than others, and parts are saltier than others. Cold, salty water is denser than warm, fresh water, so it sinks. Once the water warms up or gets diluted with less salty water, it will rise back to the surface.

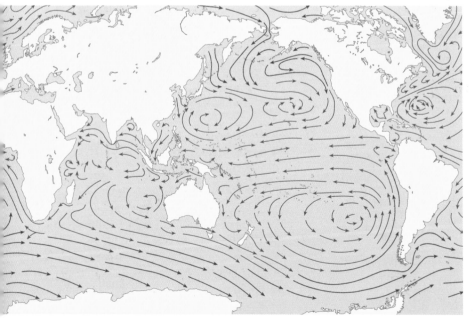

◀ This map shows the surface currents in different parts of the ocean. Currents of warm water are in red, cold currents are in blue.

▶ Atolls are coral islands that grow on the cones of underwater volcanoes. This is why atolls form in a circle. They are made from the skeletons of corals, tiny underwater animals that live together in huge numbers.

Surface currents are important because they bring warm water to cool places. For example, the Gulf Stream brings warm water from the Gulf of Mexico to Britain and the rest of north-west Europe. Without the Gulf Stream, Britain would be as cold in winter as north-east Canada. Deep currents are also important, because they bring nutrient-rich water from the bottom of the ocean up to the surface where fish feed. Because currents are driven by wind and heat, they change from season to season and when the Earth's climate changes.

Ancient water

The ocean is almost as old as Earth itself. Geologists think that when Earth first formed, it got so hot that most of it melted. Many minerals are partly made of water. When the minerals melted, water was released to the Earth's surface through volcanoes. Some volcanoes may still be spewing out water that has never been on the Earth's surface before. Another source of water could have been the comets that bombarded the Earth when it was young.

▼ A 'black smoker' – a hot spring in the dark world of the ocean floor. Scientists think that life on Earth may have first evolved round such springs deep under the oceans.

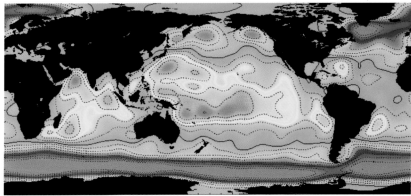

▲ A map of the height of the ocean surface compared to average sea level. Sea-surface height depends on such things as the shape of the sea floor, ocean currents, water temperature and the weather. Red indicates the highest sea levels, purple the lowest.

The ocean crust

The rocky crust beneath the oceans is quite different from the continental crust. The ocean crust is only about 10 kilometres thick (the continents are 35 kilometres thick). It is made almost entirely of the igneous (volcanic) rocks, basalt and gabbro. On top of the rocks is a layer of clay and mud made of sediments that have washed off the continents, and of skeletons of tiny sea creatures.

EBB AND FLOOD

Throughout the day, on almost every sea coast on Earth, the sea water slowly rises and falls. These rises and falls are called tides. A tide is really a wave, thousands of kilometres long.

Tides are caused by gravity, the force that attracts one object to another. Like the Earth, the Moon and the Sun both have a gravitational pull, which affects the world's oceans and seas.

The pull of the Moon

As the Moon orbits Earth, its gravity forces water into two bulges, one on the side of Earth facing the Moon and the other directly opposite. There are high tides at the two bulges and low tides in between.

As the Earth spins, places move in and out of the bulges. Most places on Earth experience at least one high tide and one low tide every day. This is because the Earth is rotating throughout the day. If you are on a beach, high tide is when the sea comes in and low tide is when it goes out. A tide is really a wave, thousands of kilometres long. On the open ocean, tidal waves travel very fast – at over 1000 km/h.

▶ Spring tides occur when the Sun and the Moon pull the sea in the same direction, making the water rise and fall more than normal. Neap tides occur when the Sun and the Moon pull the sea in different directions, so the difference between high and low tides is less.

 key words
- gravity
- Moon
- neap tide
- spring tide
- Sun
- waves

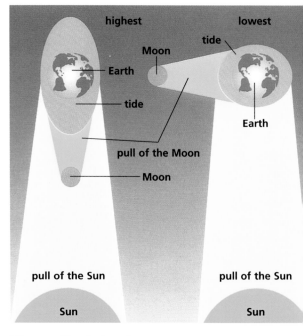

The pull of the Sun

The Sun also pulls on the water, but since the Sun is so much farther away, the pull is not as strong. The high tides are highest and the low tides lowest when the Sun and Moon are pulling in the same direction. This happens when they are on the same side of the Earth or directly opposite each other. When the Moon and Sun pull in different directions the difference between high and low tides is less.

▼ The Thames Barrier is the world's largest tidal flood barrier. It protects London from destructive and dangerous flooding which could be caused when there is a powerful storm in the North Sea at the same time as a high tide.

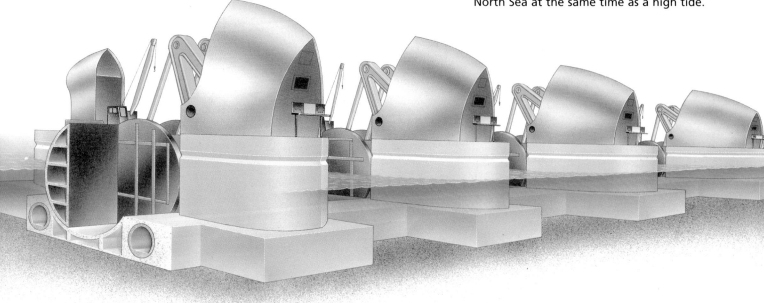

A BLANKET OF AIR

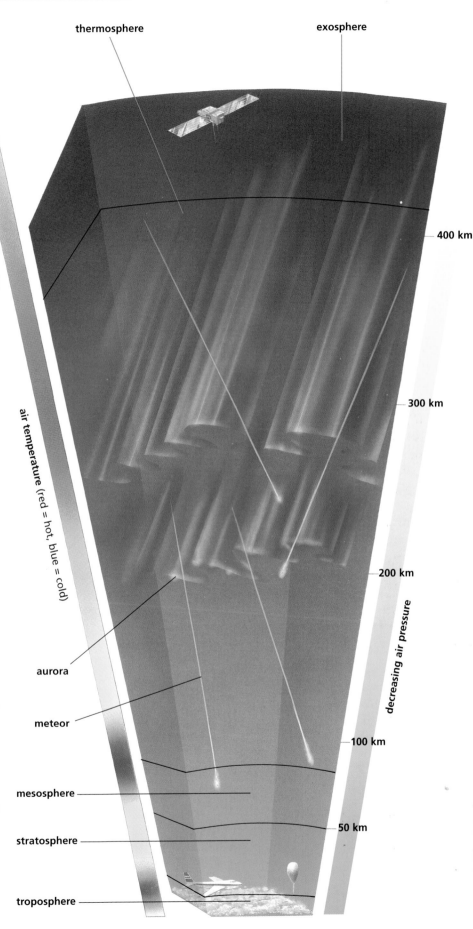

Seen from space, the Earth's atmosphere is a thin blue layer of air. Without it, the Earth would be a very different place. The atmosphere traps heat from the Sun, keeping it from escaping into space. Winds in the atmosphere carry vital rain from place to place. And two of the gases in the air, oxygen and carbon dioxide, are essential for life.

An atmosphere is a blanket of gas that surrounds a planet. Earth's atmosphere is almost 10,000 kilometres thick, but most of it is in the 30 kilometres closest to Earth.

Atmospheric pressure

Although it may not feel like it, air pushes on us from all sides. The weight of the air pushing on us is known as *atmospheric pressure*, or air pressure. As you rise in the atmosphere, there is less and less air pressing down from above, so atmospheric pressure decreases.

You can also think of air pressure as the amount of air in a certain volume of space. This idea is very important to mountain climbers and pilots. At the top of Mount Everest, at 8848 metres above sea level, a lungful of air contains less than a third as many oxygen molecules as it does at sea level. Where jets fly, 14 kilometres high, the atmospheric pressure is only 15 per cent of what it is on the ground. If we didn't pressurize airline cabins by pumping air into them, passengers would suffocate.

▶ Without an atmosphere, the Earth would be a very different planet. The atmosphere moves heat and water from place to place on Earth. It also acts like a blanket, keeping heat from escaping out into space. Oxygen and carbon dioxide gases in the atmosphere 'feed' plants and animals. Ozone gas in the upper atmosphere absorbs harmful ultraviolet light.

thermosphere

exosphere

400 km

300 km

air temperature (red = hot, blue = cold)

200 km

decreasing air pressure

aurora

meteor

100 km

mesosphere

50 km

stratosphere

troposphere

key words

- air
- air pressure
- atmosphere
- atmospheric pressure
- stratosphere

▶ View of Earth at sunset. You can see how thin the atmosphere layer is in this picture.

From the ground up

From the ground up, the atmosphere changes. In the lower atmosphere (called the *troposphere*), the air gets colder as you go higher. This is because we actually get warmth from the Earth's surface, not directly from the Sun. The Sun heats the surface, which then radiates the heat back out and warms the air.

It is also much easier to get sunburned high in the atmosphere because there are fewer air molecules to absorb and scatter the Sun's rays.

Other atmospheres

Every planet has a slightly different atmosphere. The atmosphere on Mars is mainly carbon dioxide, while that of Uranus is hydrogen and helium. Larger planets have thicker atmospheres because they have a stronger gravitational pull. Gases have a hard time escaping the gravity of a large planet like Jupiter. By contrast, the Moon is so small and its gravity is so low that it has almost no atmosphere at all.

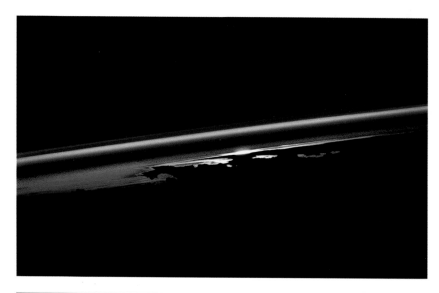

LIFE CHANGED OUR ATMOSPHERE

When Earth's atmosphere first formed over 4 billion years ago, it contained very little oxygen. No one is exactly sure what the first living things were like, but eventually they evolved into tiny simple plants. Like plants today, they made food for themselves using sunlight, water and carbon dioxide. One of the products of this food-making process was oxygen. As these organisms grew and multiplied, they changed the atmosphere, reducing the amount of carbon dioxide and increasing the amount of oxygen, eventually making it possible for oxygen-breathing animals to evolve.

Earth's atmosphere today is made mostly of nitrogen and oxygen. It also contains small amounts of other gases such as water vapour, argon, carbon dioxide and ozone. Animals need oxygen to breathe, while plants make their food from carbon dioxide.

Human beings have changed the atmosphere in only a few hundred years. For instance, through pollution we have added extra carbon dioxide which has caused global warming.

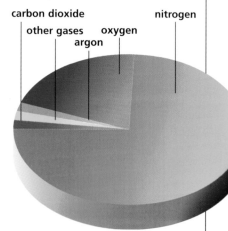

nitrogen   carbon dioxide
hydrogen

▲ Composition of Earth's early atmosphere.

carbon dioxide   nitrogen
other gases   oxygen
argon

▲ Earth's atmosphere today.

◀ Even though Venus is about the same size as Earth, Venus's atmosphere is 90 times thicker than ours. It traps heat so well that the temperature of Venus's surface is about 430 °C.

THE ATMOSPHERE TODAY

Every summer, fierce cyclones rage across tropical seas, bringing torrential rains, hurricane winds and huge waves to coastal areas. A fully-formed cyclone can be 500 kilometres across, with winds of more than 120 kilometres per hour.

Tropical cyclones are one example of the Earth's weather. Weather is the sum total of what the atmosphere is doing at a given time and place.

Weather happens in the lower 12–15 kilometres of the atmosphere, a layer called the *troposphere*. The troposphere gets its name from the Greek word 'tropo', which means swirling. Different regions of air in the troposphere are at different temperatures and carry different amounts of water. These air masses are moved around by winds and interact with each other to make the weather.

Air masses and fronts

An air mass is a large region of air that has roughly the same temperature and moisture content throughout. Air masses can be 10 kilometres high and cover millions of square kilometres. A large air mass can bring several days of dry, sunny,

▶ Weather balloons are sent up into the atmosphere to make measurements at high altitudes. They carry a number of instruments, including radar to detect rainstorms and tornadoes.

key words

- air mass
- front
- storm
- weather

breezy weather, or a few days of cloudy, rainy weather to an area.

Weather can be slightly different from place to place within an air mass. It is usually warmer in the cities than in the countryside, and cooler on top of a mountain than in a valley. The coast is usually cooler in the summer and warmer in the winter than places inland.

Most storms develop at *fronts*, where two different air masses meet. However, hurricanes, typhoons and cyclones develop within a single air mass, not along a front.

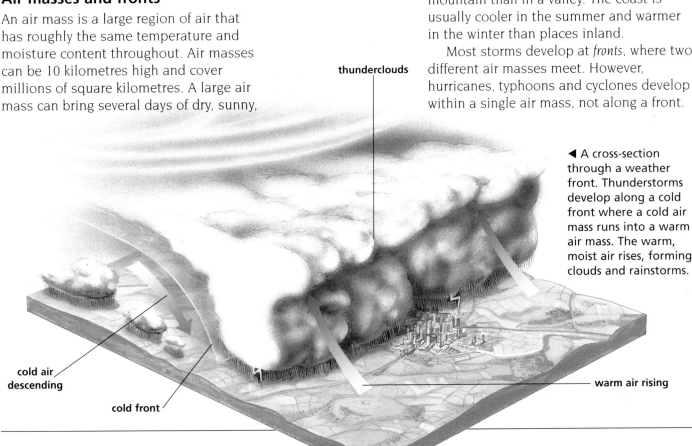

thunderclouds

◀ A cross-section through a weather front. Thunderstorms develop along a cold front where a cold air mass runs into a warm air mass. The warm, moist air rises, forming clouds and rainstorms.

cold air descending

cold front

warm air rising

Watching the weather

Meteorologists make measurements of the atmosphere all over Earth, from weather stations on land, ships at sea, jets and balloons high in the atmosphere, and from satellites thousands of kilometres above the atmosphere.

Many different instruments are used to measure the weather. Satellites are especially important because they can 'see' weather systems develop from above in places where there are no weather stations on the ground.

Predicting the weather

In order to make an accurate weather forecast, meteorologists need to have as much information about the atmosphere as possible. Once they have worked out where certain air masses are moving, they can try to predict where they will be in a few days time and how they will interact with each other.

Most weather predictions are made with computers that use mathematics and physics to imitate how the atmosphere will change in the next few days. Meteorologists also make predictions based on what has happened in the past. For instance, 'a 70

per cent chance of rain' means that seven out of ten times when the weather was like this in the past, it has turned rainy.

Predicting the weather can be extremely difficult because it is impossible to know what every particle of air is doing. Weather forecasts for the following day or two are usually quite accurate, but it is nearly impossible to predict what the weather will be like more than five days in advance.

▲ This satellite image is a combination of three images of Hurricane Andrew as it moved west over Florida, USA, in 1992. Hurricanes develop near the Equator where the ocean water is warm. As they evaporate water, the winds grow stronger.

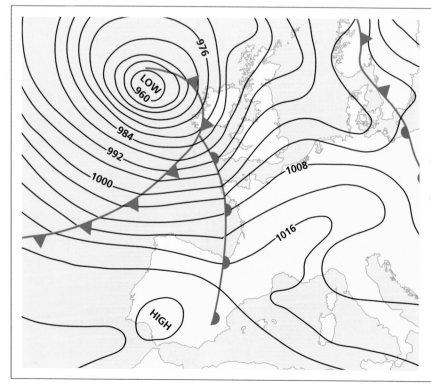

UNDERSTANDING THE WEATHER FORECAST

Weather maps like these are shown in weather forecasts every day. Some of the maps are difficult to understand, but you can get a lot of information from them, once you know what all the symbols mean.

Key

HIGH   centre of a high-pressure zone (usually dry, sunny weather)

LOW   centre of a low-pressure zone (usually cloudy and rainy weather)

1016   isobar: a line of equal air pressure in millibars

front: where two air masses meet. The notches point in the direction that the front is moving

a warm front: a warm air mass is overtaking a colder air mass

a cold front: a cold air mass is moving in to replace a warm air mass

RIVERS OF AIR

In 1492, Christopher Columbus set sail from Portugal to find a western route to India. He could not sail directly west because the winds near Portugal blow east. So he sailed south to the Canary Islands where the winds turn westward. He then sailed across the Atlantic to the Caribbean (which he thought was part of India) on the trade winds blowing west. On his return to Portugal, he sailed north until the winds turned eastward again, taking him home.

The winds that carried Columbus across the Atlantic are part of a worldwide system of winds. Wind is moving air.

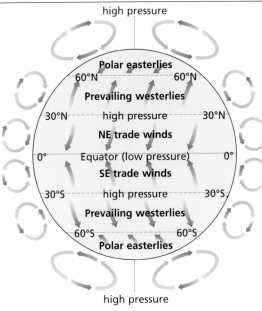

▲ This map shows the major wind belts on Earth's surface. The wind direction can change from day to day, but overall it tends to blow in one direction.

Why air moves

When you pump up a tyre, you force a lot more air into the tyre than there is in the same amount of space outside the tyre. The air pressure is higher inside the tyre than outside it. If you puncture the tyre, the air will pour out until the pressure inside is the same as on the outside.

The same thing happens in the atmosphere. There are zones of high pressure and zones of low pressure in the atmosphere (these are the 'highs' and 'lows' you see on weather maps). Just as water flows from high ground to low ground, air flows from areas of high pressure to areas of low pressure, and causes winds. The greater the difference in air pressure, the stronger the winds that are produced.

▼ On the coast there is a daily pattern to the wind. A cool sea breeze blows in from the ocean during the day, while at night the winds blow from the land to the sea. This happens because the land heats up and cools down more quickly than the sea.

▲ The winds in a tornado are the fastest in the world. They can reach up to 500 km/h.

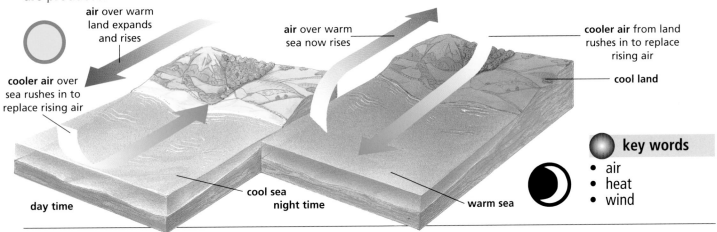

air over warm land expands and rises

cooler air over sea rushes in to replace rising air

day time

cool sea

air over warm sea now rises

night time

warm sea

cooler air from land rushes in to replace rising air

cool land

key words
- air
- heat
- wind

WATER'S NEVER-ENDING JOURNEY

Every year, about 420 million billion litres of water disappear from the ocean into the atmosphere. If the water never returned, the ocean would dry up in 2500 years. But the water forms clouds, and then rains back into the ocean and on the land.

The rain on land flows down rivers, sinks into the ground, or rises up into the atmosphere again. Eventually all the water makes its way back to the ocean.

The journey of water from the oceans to the atmosphere and back to the sea again is called the water cycle.

Solid, liquid, gas

Water can move around very quickly because it can change easily from a solid or liquid to a gas, and back again.

When water evaporates (changes from a liquid into a gas) into the atmosphere, it can travel in the air all around the world. When the water vapour in the atmosphere condenses (turns from a gas back into a liquid), it forms tiny water droplets, which make clouds. These float over the land and

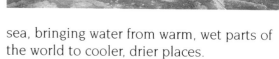

▶ On Earth, water exists as a solid (ice), a liquid and a gas (invisible water vapour in the air). This photograph of the Ilulissat ice fjord in Greenland shows water in liquid and solid state.

🔵 key words

- evaporation
- precipitation
- water

▶ Most of the water on Earth is in the oceans and most of the fresh water on Earth is frozen in glaciers and ice sheets.

sea, bringing water from warm, wet parts of the world to cooler, drier places.

Water that rises into the atmosphere from the ocean may return in hours, or it may sink into the rocks and take millions of years to return.

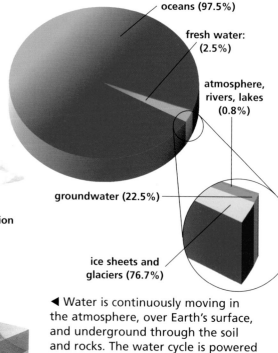

oceans (97.5%)

fresh water: (2.5%)

atmosphere, rivers, lakes (0.8%)

groundwater (22.5%)

ice sheets and glaciers (76.7%)

◀ Water is continuously moving in the atmosphere, over Earth's surface, and underground through the soil and rocks. The water cycle is powered by the Sun and by gravity. The heat of the Sun melts ice and evaporates water. Gravity makes rain and snow fall to the ground and it makes rivers flow from the mountains to the sea.

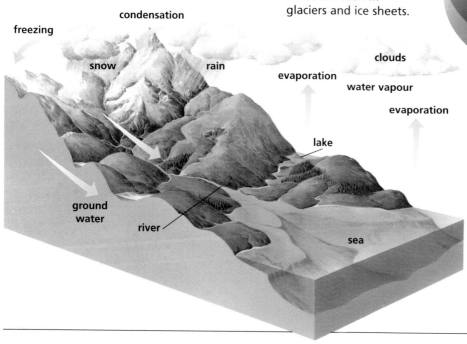

condensation

freezing

snow

rain

clouds

evaporation

water vapour

evaporation

lake

ground water

river

sea

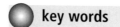

WATER IN THE SKY

The view of Earth from space is always changing. Swirling white patterns move over the surface, hiding then revealing the lands and oceans beneath. These patterns are clouds.

Clouds are made of water droplets, ice crystals, particles of dust, and air.

How clouds form

The lower part of Earth's atmosphere is full of water vapour. We can't see the water in the air because water vapour is a gas. Clouds form when some of this water vapour condenses (becomes liquid) and forms tiny water droplets. If the air is cold

▶ This photograph, taken on a space shuttle flight, shows clouds in the Earth's atmosphere.

▼ Different kinds of clouds have different shapes and form at different heights in the atmosphere.

enough, the water will form ice crystals instead of droplets.

Dust is a very important ingredient in clouds. In the air there are salt particles from the oceans, ash particles from volcanoes, tiny bits of rock and soil blown off the continents, and soot particles from factories. The particles attract water molecules and give them a place to gather into droplets. Without dust, it would be difficult for clouds to form.

Why clouds form

The main reason clouds form is because the air cools down. Warm air can hold more water vapour than cold air. When the air cools, some of the water vapour condenses and makes clouds.

Exactly how cold the air has to be before a cloud forms depends on how much water there is in the air. The less water vapour there is in the air, the colder the air has to be to form a cloud. This is why, on a dry day, the clouds are high in the sky, where it's coldest.

KEY
1 cirrus
2 cirrocumulus
3 altocumulus
4 altostratus
5 cumulonimbus
6 stratus
7 cumulus

🔵 **key words**
- atmosphere
- clouds
- water

RAINDROPS AND SNOWFLAKES

Every summer, India, Bangladesh and the rest of southern Asia are drenched by the rains of the summer monsoon. Warm, moist air blows in from the Indian Ocean and brings hundreds of centimetres of rain to the mountains and plains.

Rain falls when clouds can no longer hold their moisture. Clouds are made of water vapour, tiny water droplets, ice crystals and dust. If the droplets and crystals are very small and far apart, the air holds them up. But if the droplets are close together, they start to join. Eventually the droplets become too big and heavy to stay up in the cloud, and fall as rain.

Cooling clouds

The main reason why rain falls from clouds is because the clouds cool off. This happens when they rise higher up in the atmosphere, perhaps because the clouds are warmer than the air around them, or in order to get over a mountain.

When the air cools, the water vapour in the clouds condenses (turns to liquid) and droplets form. The same thing happens on a can of cold drink on a hot day, when water vapour from the air condenses and forms water droplets on the side of the can.

Snow, sleet and hail

Most clouds contain ice crystals as well as water droplets. As the air cools, the ice crystals grow, until they get so big that they fall to the ground. If the air is less than 0 °C all the way from the cloud to the ground, we get snow.

Sleet forms when raindrops partly freeze as they fall to the ground. Hail forms in storm clouds, when a piece of dust gets covered in layers of ice. The hailstone may grow by being blown back up into the cloud and covered in more ice. This can happen again and again, until sometimes the hailstones grow as big as golf balls!

▲ As water droplets fall through a cloud they gradually gather even more droplets. A falling raindrop would be made up of about one million droplets.

key words
- clouds
- condensation
- droplets
- hail
- rain
- sleet
- snow

▶ The monsoon rains in India. Although the monsoon causes flooding that is sometimes disastrous, the people living in monsoon regions rely on the rains. The monsoon rains water their crops, and the floods add important materials and minerals to the soil.

A HUNDRED MILLION VOLTS

Within a towering storm cloud 18 kilometres up in the air, the winds reach 100 kilometres per hour. Gusts of cold air swoop downwards, while warm, moist air shoots up. As the air churns violently, water droplets and ice crystals collide. Electrical charges build up, then suddenly a brilliant flash of lightning brightens the sky.

Lightning happens when hundreds of millions of volts of electricity flow between thunderclouds and the ground.

Lightning strikes

During a thunderstorm, the base of the thundercloud has a negative electrical charge and the ground has a positive charge. If two places have opposite electrical charges, electricity tries to flow between them to even out the charges. Electricity can move easily through materials like metal, but it has trouble moving through air. Air acts like a dam on a river, keeping the electricity from flowing. In a thunderstorm, the electrical charges build up so much, that the 'dam' of air breaks, and a bolt of 100 million volts of electricity rushes between the clouds and the ground.

▶ In a storm, electric charges build up in clouds and on the ground (a). Between them is an insulating layer of air. If the charges get big enough (b), lightning breaks through this insulating layer (c).

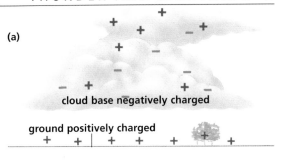
(a)
cloud base negatively charged
ground positively charged

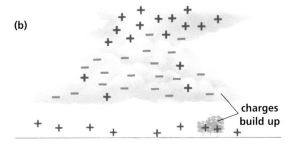
(b)
charges build up

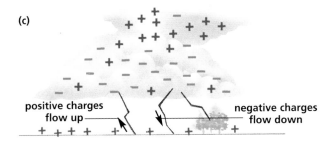
(c)
positive charges flow up
negative charges flow down

Since there are different electrical charges within the clouds, lightning can also happen within a single cloud or from cloud to cloud. This sheet lightning causes a bright flash across the sky. Heat lightning is just the light from lightning just over the horizon that is reflected off clouds.

Thunder

Whenever you hear thunder, you can be sure there is lightning somewhere. As a lightning bolt travels through the air, it instantly heats the air around it to more than 30,000°C. When air is heated, the molecules move apart and the air expands. Lightning makes the air expand so quickly that it creates a sound wave – thunder. Light travels so quickly that we see lightning as it is happening, even if it's very far away. Sound, on the other hand, travels a million times more slowly. It takes thunder about three seconds to travel a distance of one kilometre.

key words
- clouds
- electricity
- lightning
- storms
- thunder

◀ Lightning bolts are huge surges of static electricity that run between clouds and from clouds to the ground.

PATTERNS IN THE WEATHER

Six thousand years ago, the Sahara was a lush grassland watered by the summer rains. Crocodiles and hippos lived in the rivers and lakes while giraffes, elephants and cattle grazed on the savannah. Slowly the climate changed and the Sahara dried out. It is now the largest desert on Earth.

Climate is the average weather of a particular place over many years. Although the weather can change from day to day, and even during a single day, climate stays the same for many years.

Climate zones

Different parts of the world have different climates. Land is grouped into particular climate zones according to its average temperature, how much rain and snow fall, and how much the weather changes from season to season. Since plants depend so much on temperature, sunshine, and rainfall, each climate also tends to have its own typical vegetation.

What makes climate

The main reason that some places are warmer than others is because different places on Earth receive different amounts of the Sun's energy. The tropics are warm because the Sun shines almost directly overhead all year long. The Arctic and Antarctic are cold because they receive less sunlight over the year.

Water absorbs and gives out the Sun's energy more slowly than the land, so places near the coast have more even climates than places in the middle of a continent. Climates are also affected by ocean currents. Some currents bring warm water, and warm, rainy weather. Others bring cold water, and cool, dry weather.

tropical: warm and humid

- rain all year
- monsoon (short dry season, long wet season)
- dry winters

hot desert: dry

- no reliable rain
- a little rain

temperate

- no dry season
- dry winters

mountain

☐ temperature and rainfall depend on height

CONSTRUCTING PAST CLIMATES

We can learn about climates far in the past by looking at things like rocks, ice and trees. For instance, salt forms in hot, dry climates, so a layer of salt in a rock formation is evidence that the climate was hot and dry when the rocks were formed. A layer of boulders and gravel left by a glacier is evidence of a cold climate.

Every season, trees add a new ring of growth to their trunks. The thickness of the ring depends on the climate and how good the growing conditions were.

In the section of part of a tree shown below, the thinner rings may have formed when the climate was cooler or drier than when the thick rings formed.

◄ This map shows the world's major climate zones. Within each zone there are smaller differences. For instance, mountains are generally cooler than low areas, and cities are always warmer than the countryside.

Winds affect the climate, too. Winds can bring warm air to cold places, for example, or moist air to dry places.

Climate change

Although climate often stays the same over many years, it does slowly change. Over thousands of years, continents move, ocean currents change and wind patterns change.

Climate also changes when the atmosphere changes. Some scientists think that the Earth was so warm 50 million years ago because the atmosphere contained more greenhouse gases (such as carbon dioxide), which trapped more heat.

Powerful volcanic eruptions can cool climates for a few years. In 1815, Tambora volcano erupted, sending clouds of ash and gas into the atmosphere. The clouds reduced the amount of sunlight reaching the Earth, and the climate was cooler.

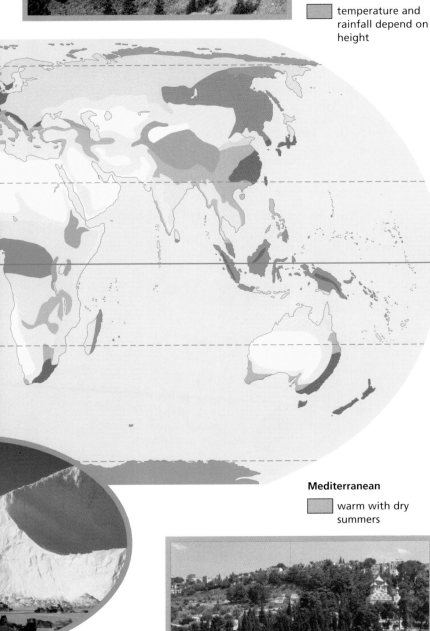

Mediterranean

☐ warm with dry summers

polar region: cold

☐ rain all year

☐ dry winters

☐ polar, dry all year

THE YEARLY CYCLE

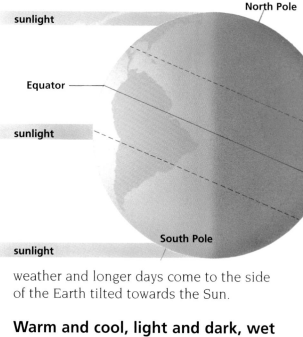

sunlight

North Pole

Equator

sunlight

sunlight

South Pole

In the middle of June in the Arctic Circle, the Sun is still out at 2 am. It hasn't dipped below the horizon since March and it won't until September. At the South Pole, in Antarctica, it has been dark for three months and the Sun won't rise for another three.

The temperature, weather and amount of daylight change with the seasons, throughout the year and from place to place. These changes are all to do with the Earth's yearly journey around the Sun.

Earth moving through space

The Earth is tilted on its axis, and the way it is tilted affects the amount of sunlight different areas receive. Between mid-March and mid-September the North Pole leans towards the Sun, and the South Pole leans away from it. From mid-September to mid-March, the reverse is true. Warmer

▶ Winter is colder than summer because there is less sunlight. The days are shorter and the Sun is lower in the sky. When the Sun is low in the sky, less of its energy reaches the Earth's surface.

 key words

- axis
- orbit
- season

weather and longer days come to the side of the Earth tilted towards the Sun.

Warm and cool, light and dark, wet and dry

Seasons are different in different parts of the world. In temperate latitudes (mid-way between the Equator and the poles), there are four very different seasons: winter, spring, summer and autumn. Near the North and South Poles there are just two seasons: a light season and a dark season, and it stays cool all year.

In the tropics, near the Equator, it is hot all year round, because the Sun is always high in the sky. But many regions near the Equator have a rainy season in the summer and a dry season in the winter.

◀ The Earth takes a year to make one orbit around the Sun. From mid-March to mid-September, the North Pole is tilted towards the Sun, and it is warmer in the northern hemisphere. From mid-September to mid-March the South Pole is tilted towards the Sun, and it is warmer in the south.

▼ This time-lapse photograph shows the position of the Sun at one-hour intervals throughout the day near the North Pole in midsummer. Although the Sun dips very low, it never actually sets.

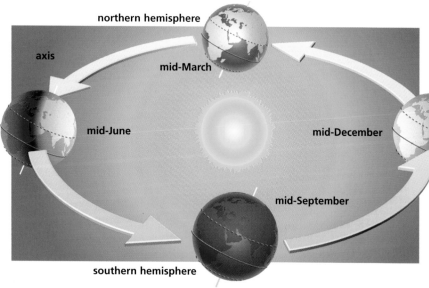

northern hemisphere

axis

mid-March

mid-June

mid-December

mid-September

southern hemisphere

GETTING HOTTER

Scientists estimate that the Earth's surface is warming up by 1°C every 40 years. Two and a half degrees in one century might not sound like much, but it is at least 50 times faster than any climate change in the past 10,000 years.

Earth's climate changes naturally, but the global warming of the last century can't be explained by natural processes alone. Most global warming is probably caused by our pollution of the environment.

The greenhouse effect

The Earth's surface absorbs sunlight and turns it into heat. Some of this heat escapes into space, but some is absorbed by gases such as carbon dioxide and water vapour in the atmosphere. These gases are known as 'greenhouse gases' because they act like the glass of a greenhouse, letting sunlight in, but not letting heat out.

Without the natural greenhouse effect, the Earth's surface would be too cold for anything to live on. The problem is that people are polluting the atmosphere with extra greenhouse gases. The gases build up in the atmosphere and trap more and more heat.

Effects of global warming

It is impossible to know exactly what will happen if it keeps getting warmer, but global warming will certainly change weather patterns. More ocean water will evaporate and create more rain, causing flooding in coastal areas. More water will evaporate from the land, leaving many places drier. As the climates change, some plants and animals will migrate into new areas, but others will die out.

The results of global warming could be disastrous. But there are many things we can do to slow global warming down, such as using less electricity, recycling rubbish, and walking or cycling instead of driving.

▶ Ice calving (breaking off) from the Childs glacier, Alaska, USA. Global warming is causing glaciers and ice sheets to melt at both the North and South Poles.

key words
- climate change
- global warming
- greenhouse effect

Global warming will make sea levels rise, causing coastal areas to flood and contaminating fresh water supplies with salt water. Many islands in the Pacific will be drowned completely.

▼ Many different things contribute to the greenhouse effect. As well as burning fuels and releasing chemicals into the air, humans have cut down many forests. Plants absorb carbon dioxide, so the loss of trees increases the levels of this greenhouse gas.

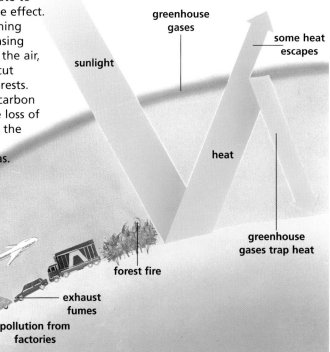

sunlight

greenhouse gases

some heat escapes

heat

greenhouse gases trap heat

forest fire

exhaust fumes

pollution from factories

GLOSSARY

This glossary gives simple explanations of difficult or specialist words that readers might be unfamiliar with. Words in *italic* have their own glossary entry.

atmosphere   The layer of gases around a planet.

atom   The smallest particle of an *element*.

compound   A substance made of two or more different *elements*.

condensation   The process of turning a gas into a liquid.

continent   A large landmass. Continents include land above water as well as continental shelves, which are under water.

core   The centre layer of the Earth; the core is divided into the liquid outer core and the solid inner core.

crust   The rocky outer layer of the Earth. Ocean crust makes up the ocean floors and continental crust makes up the *continents*.

crystal   A solid material with atoms arranged in a geometric pattern. All *minerals* form crystals.

current   A mass of moving water within the ocean.

deposit   (1) A layer of *sediment*. (2) An accumulation of an important *mineral* or *element* in a rock, for example gold.

element   One of the simple substances that make up matter. Each element is made of only one kind of *atom*.

erosion   The process by which rocks are gradually broken down and moved from one place to another, by ice, rivers, rain or wind.

evaporation   The process of turning a liquid into a gas.

evolution   The gradual development, over many generations, of plants and animals into new forms of life.

fossil   The remains of a living thing preserved in rock.

geology   The study of the structure of the Earth's crust and its layers.

glacier   A thick mass of ice and snow that flows slowly downhill or sideways under its own weight.

global warming   The warming-up of the Earth's surface as a result of the *greenhouse effect*.

gravity   The force that attracts two objects. Earth's gravity keeps everything on Earth from floating out to space. It makes things flow downhill and fall to the ground.

greenhouse effect   The way in which gases in the Earth's atmosphere help to keep the Earth warm enough for life to survive. These 'greenhouse gases' act like glass in a greenhouse, letting sunlight in but not letting heat out. Pollution adds to the gases, trapping too much heat and causing *global warming*.

igneous rock   A rock that forms when hot, liquid rock called *magma* turns solid. Granite is an example of igneous rock.

latitude   The distance north or south of the Equator. Latitude is measured in degrees: the Equator is at 0°, the North Pole is 90° N, and the South Pole is 90° S.

lava   Hot, liquid rock on the Earth's surface; a type of *magma*.

longitude   The distance of a place east or west of the Prime Meridian. Longitude is measured in degrees. The Prime Meridian, at 0°, is a line that runs from the North Pole to the South Pole, through Greenwich, England.

magma   Hot, liquid rock.

mantle   The hot, rocky layer of the Earth between the *crust* and the *core*.

metamorphic rock   A rock that has been transformed into a new rock by being naturally heated and/or squeezed. Coal and gneiss are metamorphic rocks.

mineral   A natural solid material that has a specific chemical composition and a definite crystalline structure. Salt and quartz are minerals.

molecule   A group of two or more *atoms* bonded to each other.

plate tectonics   The theory that the Earth's surface is made of about a dozen moving pieces called plates. Their movement forms and shapes features such as *continents*, mountains and ocean floors.

sediment   Small, loose pieces of broken rocks or dead organisms. Sand, shells and peat are all sediments.

sedimentary rock   A rock made of loose *sediments* that have hardened into solid rock. Limestone and sandstone are sedimentary rocks.

seismology   The scientific study and recording of earthquakes.

volcanic rock   A type of *igneous rock* that forms when *lava* turns solid. Basalt is an example of volcanic rock.

weathering   The process of a rock or mineral decaying or falling apart.

INDEX

Page numbers in **bold** mean that this is where you will find the most information on that subject. If both a heading and a page number are in bold, there is an article with that title. A page number in *italic* means that there is a picture of that subject. There may also be other information about the subject on the same page.

ACKNOWLEDGEMENTS

Key
t = top; c = centre; b = bottom; r = right; l = left; back = background; fore = foreground

Artwork
Baker, Julian: 44 cl. **Birkett, Georgie:** 37 tl. **D'Achille, Gino:** 15 cr. **Farmer, Andrew:** 11 t; 13 b; 15 tr; 18 b; 20–21 t; 35 b; 37 b. **Franklin, Mark:** 32 b; 35 tr. **Full Steam Ahead:** 12–13 t; 19 cr; 34 br; 38 cr. **Gary Hincks:** 10 t; 20 bl; 23 t; 25 b; 26 b; 27 t; 29 br; 38 bl; 39 bl. **Learoyd, Tracey:** 16 t; 19 b; 30 cr, bl; 36 b; 37 tr. **Oxford University Press:** 6 tr; 7 tl, b; 21 br; 42–43 c. **Saunders, Michael:** 4 b; 5 b; 12 tr; 14 cr; 17 cl; 24 b; 28 b; 29 tr; 33 cr; 40 tr; 41 tr; 44 tr; 45 br. **Visscher, Peter:** 6 tl; 8 tl; 9 tl; 10 tl; 12 tl; 14 tl; 15 tl; 18 tl; 19 tl; 20 tl; 22 tl; 24 tl; 25 tl; 26 tl; 28 tl; 29 tl; 30 tl; 32 tl; 33 tl; 35 tl; 38 tl; 39 tl; 40 tl; 41 tl; 42 tl; 44 tl.

Photos
The publishers would like to thank the following for permission to use their photographs.

Clerk, Sir John, of Penicuik: 8 b.
Corbis: 18 tr (Galen Rowell); 24 tr (Charles & Josette Lenars); 43 tl.
Corel: 42 c; 42–43 bc; 43 bc, br.
Edwards, Professor Dianne, Department of Earth Sciences, Cardiff, UK: 13 tc.
ESA: 31 cr (Near-Earth Navigation & Geodesy).
Liverpool Geological Society: 6 bl.
NASA: 4 tr (Goddard Space Flight Center, data from NOAA GOES); 23 br (JPL/Malin Space Science Systems); 26 cr (JPL); 34 tr; 34 bl (JPL); 36 tr (Goddard Space Flight Center, data from NOAA GOES).
NOAA/NGDC/Peter W. Sloss: 5 tr.
Oxford University Museum of Natural History: 9 bl, br, cl; 10 c, cr; 12 tr.
Oxford University Press: 9 tr; 10 cl; 13 cr.
Panos Pictures: 22 tr (Alfredo Cedeno).
Photodisc: 4 tl; 39 tr.
Planet Earth Pictures: 30 tr (Jason Child).
Robert Harding: 40 b (J. H. C. Wilson).

Schopf, J. W.: 12 cr.
Science Photo Library: 8 cr (Hank Morgan); 10 tr (George Bernard); 13 tr (Mark Pilkington/Geological Survey of Canada); 13 cr (John Reader); 13 tl; 14 bl (Sinclair Stammers); 15 b (Bill Bachman); 19 tr (David Parker); 20 cr (Gregory Dimijian); 21 cl (CNES, 1988 Distribution Spot Image); 22 b (John Mead); 25 tr (Noburu Komine); 27 br (David Nunuk); 28 tr (Baerbel K. Luccitta/US Geological Survey); 31 bl (Dr Ken MacDonald); 31 tr (Douglas Faulkner); 37 cr (E. R. Degginger); 38 tr (Bernhard Edmaier); 41 bl (Kent Wood); 42 tr (Simon Fraser); 43 tr (Adam Hart-Davis); 45 tr (Bernhard Edmaier).
Scotese, C. R.: 16 b (PALEOMAP Project, University of Texas at Arlington (www.scotese.com)).
Small, Christopher, Lamont Doherty Earth Observatory, Columbia University, USA: 45 tl.
Sterner, Ray, Johns Hopkins University Applied Physics Laboratory: 7 tr (US Geological Survey).
stone: 44 b.